HAUNTED
WORCESTERSHIRE

HAUNTED
WORCESTERSHIRE

ANTHONY POULTON-SMITH

First published 2009

The History Press
The Mill, Brimscombe Port
Stroud, Gloucestershire, GL5 2QG
www.thehistorypress.co.uk

British Library Cataloguing in Publication Data.
A catalogue record for this book is available from the British Library.

ISBN 978 0 7524 4872 5

Typesetting and origination by The History Press
Printed in Great Britain

CONTENTS

Author's Note

My second literary excursion into the subject of ghosts has been every bit as pleasurable as my first (detailed in *Black Country Ghosts*). When reading the following narratives you will note there are recurring references to three particular eras in the history of Worcestershire – the Roman occupation, the English Civil War, and the days of the stagecoach. While there has been many undoubted links between Worcestershire and the English Civil War, this does not explain why there are so many hauntings from this short period of time – no more than ten years covering the whole conflict.

These stories were related by a county of warm and friendly individuals who can certainly be relied upon to make a welcoming cup of tea or coffee. While many a comfortable overnight room prevented long hours being wasted journeying from my native Staffordshire.

To those who provided a tale, a lead (or a cuppa!) goes my heartfelt thanks, for without you this would have been a very short book indeed. Thanks also to the libraries and librarians and staff at the record offices, who showed considerable patience in assisting with my endeavours. My gratitude also goes to those who corrected a traditional tale and pointed out the errors and inaccuracies, and also to the many who pointed a very lost author in the right direction. For those who allowed me to photograph their homes, churches, roads, pubs, businesses, fields and gardens; the many who gave up precious moments of their busy lives either in person or by tying up their telephone line; and to all those who contributed by revealing some of their most personal experiences I shall always be most grateful.

This book contains over 120 different sightings and experiences. Thus it occurs to me that, from a personal perspective, I am missing out on a whole world which is just waiting to be written down. If these are just the ones that I have found out about for this book, imagine how many more are out there awaiting my discovery. Indeed if I could detect or even talk to these memories of times gone by directly, it would produce a number of sequels – so watch this space!

INTRODUCTION

Having produced a book on the ghosts of the Black Country, I was anxious to continue to explore the unexplained phenomena elsewhere. It did not take much thought before deciding that Worcestershire should be my next target.

Anyone who has read my earlier book on ghosts will know I have yet to be convinced of their existence; my personal experiences are limited to a mere split second. Driving along a trunk road at about 9 p.m. one very autumnal weekday I was about to enter the outskirts of Lichfield. Being well-acquainted with the road I was already allowing the car to slow in anticipation of the reduced speed limits when the headlights fell on a region of mist lying across the road. At this time of year a bank of mist in this particular spot was almost predictable, the natural landscape had created a small seasonal brook, effectively little more than a drainage ditch. There are a couple of long-established buildings on one side of the road and nothing but agricultural land on the other, thus I was surprised to see a coachman driving his team of horses at breakneck speed across the road.

If such apparitions are memories of past events then we would expect to find an old road around here. Yet there has not been a road across here for the last 2,000 years, and the image was only dating from about 200 years ago. Furthermore, if this was a glimpse of the old stagecoach days, they would have been travelling at a speed not yet attained by the fastest modern train service! Having always dismissed the comments of others as misinterpretations of their personal experiences this occurrence forced me to rethink. Hence I concluded, rightly or wrongly, that I was mistaken – particularly since researching this and the previous book on ghosts has shown me that many feel it is necessary to be attuned to such phenomena.

Irrespective of my opinions there are many who have some wondrous stories to tell from personal experience. Narratives of events which have affected their lives to some degree are related from a unique and highly personal perspective and have provided me with the opportunity to meet many friendly and engaging individuals. Thus I travelled in search of more stories and pointed the car to the south-west in the direction of Worcester and the Malverns. Having crossed swords with the county a number of times in my life, including when writing *Worcestershire Place Names* and *Ley Lines Across the Midlands*, I already had some knowledge of the ghosts reported within the shire. It did not take long to find great diversity in the reports, be they well known and reported previously or brand new stories never before seen in print.

As with most regions, there are a number of reports from public houses. Whether this is due to the strength or volume of the drink consumed is uncertain. Maybe the reason is simply because these places are frequented by a good cross-section of the locals and often after dark. Public houses can often be among the oldest established properties in an area, along with churches which are another popular locale, which has long made them frequently mentioned when giving directions. Other obvious haunted locations include castles and stately homes. Again they have been occupied and have stood for a very long time. However, we also find very recent buildings, notably new homes, where phenomena have appeared which cannot possibly have anything to do with the present building.

Not only is every kind of building is covered within this book, but people and creatures from every walk of life; from aristocrats to the lowliest servant, the elderly, children, men, women, the most faithful pet and the wildest animal.

Not all the tales are told by those who were frightened by their experience, indeed few of the experiences can be considered to have been malevolent. Many of those I spoke to were indifferent, some even considered it amusing, and a few remain sceptical of what they had seen. Yet the majority agreed they were simply unable to give any other explanation for what they had seen, heard or felt other than it being a ghost.

Anthony Poulton-Smith, 2009

A–Z OF HAUNTED WORCESTERSHIRE

ABBERLEY

Manor Arms

Visiting the delightful Manor Arms hotel was one of the highlights of my journey across the county. The main body of the pub dates from 1580, while the area away from the main bar area is even older. It was once the local court (the police station was opposite across the village square), a name telling of its former importance. Peter, who has owned the property for several years now, explained there was a tunnel linking the court house and police station, allowing criminals to be transported without fear of them being freed by their friends.

The ghost here is the Grey Lady, so-called for the drab colouring of her flowing garments. While the hotel is the centre of the attention, she also wanders elsewhere in the village, routinely crossing the village square on her walks. Just who she is and what connects her to Abberley and the Manor Arms is unknown. Her clothes date her to somewhere around the Stuart or Georgian periods of English history, yet this has not helped to uncover any likely identity. She does not appear forlorn or anxious – unlike many ghostly ladies – indeed she appears blissfully unaware of modern life, calmly walking around the village without a care in the world.

One day in 2006 a couple stopped at the hotel for a night. They were given room number six, the Manor Suite. The next morning they hurried downstairs, anxious to show Peter two digital photographs they had taken mere moments apart. While in the room they had been aware, as had previous occupiers of the room, of an inexplicable chill. They had noticed a bizarre mist forming over the four-poster bed, a ball of eddying wisps about 18in in diameter, and had taken two photographs of it. When they examined the images later they discovered that, while the image was present both times the photographs were taken, it only appeared on the digital image once, the second was completely clear.

Was the spirit of Abberley suddenly camera shy?

ABBERTON

Bransil Castle

The old moat of Bransil Castle is reputedly guarded by a ghostly crow. This large, long-lived black bird defends the castle against all-comers until the rightful owner, as seen through its eyes, is found.

The Manor Arms remains the focal point of Abberley.

Built in the fifteenth century, although known as a castle, it is effectively a manor house with a gatehouse and a moat. Originally the property of Lord Beauchamp of Powick, it passed down the line until it came to a Mr Reed of Herefordshire, who took steps to claim the title, but died before his right to the peerage could be considered.

Next in line was Mrs Sheldon, sister of the deceased, then her son and ultimately his wife who lived at Abberton. Along with the potential title and lands came possession of a small box. The box held the remains of the first Lord Beauchamp and was also the repository for his spirit.

At the castle the bird continued to guard the moat and the fabled chest of money reputedly hidden therein. It was said that only the rightful heir to the title and the lands could claim and get their hands on the treasure, providing they also held the spirit of Lord Beauchamp. Today, the moat has been filled in and the remains of the building have been steadily crumbling for over two centuries, leaving little standing.

If the crow still protects the treasure it has the perfect disguise, blending in with the other crows, rooks and ravens seen in the English countryside every day. Furthermore, it seems the bird is still doing its job as well as ever, for no trace of the treasure has ever been discovered.

ALVECHURCH

Bordesley Hall

This story from the ancient estate of Bordesley Hall, in the very north of the county, was related by John Haynes, the owner and a man who has been associated with the place as long as anyone. Today the original building has been surrounded by an array of newer buildings and offices, providing quality business premises in as lovely surroundings as any employee could wish to find.

To find the beginnings of Bordesley Park we have to travel back 800 years, when the land was owned by the Abbey of Bordesley and the annual rent was paid to the Rector of Alvechurch. All was quiet until the sixteenth century, when the Abbey was ravaged under the orders of Henry VIII, a period of English history known as the Dissolution of the Monasteries – a title which hides the simple fact that the King was wresting power from the Catholic Church and holding it himself as he broke away from Rome and the papacy.

The modern story of the park starts in 1561 when Lord Windsor marked out 1,000 acres. This was effectively one large farm and by the time it had passed into the hands of the Foleys, the Dugdales, and Mr Wiggin it was a sizable and profitable farm. It was during this period that the present house was built. In 1941 the final owner, Mr Patrick, broke the land up into smaller parcels and sold it off. This eventually resulted in the business centre we see today.

This long history has resulted in various unexplained events and a number of evenings have been arranged to investigate and experience these phenomena. John Haynes himself was one of a group, consisting of seven men and four women, which returned to Bordesley Hall one evening. The rooms are sizable and occupied by various businesses, and it was when they were in the Rose Garden room that the first incident was reported. A number of the group claimed to be psychic and could detect visitors from beyond the grave; these were in addition to the medium, who lead the group in the search for the often reported White Lady.

John Haynes, who was acting as caretaker on this particular evening, had joined the party but remained away from the main group, being seated towards the rear of the 30m by 20m room. One of the men called out there was a presence by the door. John looked around but could see nothing except a man seated just in front of him about 3m to his left and another 4m away to his right. He ignored the claim as nobody else seemed to agree until another cried out that he, too, could sense a presence. As before John looked around and could see nothing but the same two men. It was then that he had a brainwave and decided to conduct a head count. At the beginning there had been seven men and four women, however now there was an extra man. He checked and rechecked his count and then realised the man to his right, by the door, had vanished.

John kept this information to himself and continued on the tour with the group. They formed a ring and 'reached out' to any watching presence again and again around the ground floor, but to no avail, and so headed to the first floor and formed a ring.

Bordesley Hall, Alvechurch is now a business centre.

As they did so a palpable icy chill passed through the area, although no door or window was open and the night was virtually still. As they seated themselves John was astonished to see a number of green glowing lights appear in the centre of the circle. These were no ordinary lights, being described as beautiful and similar to the soft luminescence of the light from optical fibres. Saying nothing, John turned his head from side to side to see if it was a trick of the light or a reflection, but this was not possible for the lights did not move. Furthermore, as he leaned to the side and allowed the head of the man alongside him to pass into his field of view the lights were obstructed.

As he watched, the green points of light became blurred and moved across to one side of the circle. Obscured from John's view he could not see what had become of the lights, but the man they had come to rest in front of was showing distress. He resisted calls for the circle to be broken but called out again and again that there was something at his throat. Eventually the lights returned to the centre of the circle and the man became calm once more. As the lights blinked out, leaving the place in darkness, they discussed what had happened. John, who had not yet said anything of what he had seen, listened as half the party reported seeing lights while the remainder saw nothing. The medium, who had remained silent throughout, informed them that either a man had hanged himself in that room or someone had witnessed a hanging while standing in that room.

As they continued on the tour John was reminded of a colleague who claimed to have heard music while locking up. Indeed several times he had searched room after room for the supposed radio which had been left on after everyone had left, without success.

It was then that the medium asked if anyone else could hear a piano playing. Three or four others said they, too, could hear an unrecognised tune being picked out on a piano.

Earlier that day the medium had been taken on a tour of the estate around the main building. She had stopped at one corner and said she sensed rotting flesh, not human flesh, but that of a horse. Furthermore she also said she could sense a man in jodhpurs leading a horse out of the thicket. She seemed unsurprised to hear this had been a cemetery for animals, mostly favoured pets, and had been untouched for so long it was, and still is, hidden beneath a well-nigh impenetrable blanket of vegetation.

Alongside the pet cemetery had once stood a tree, a Cedar of Lebanon, which had been planted to commemorate the victory at the Battle of Blenheim. That tree had crashed to the ground in a storm and a new one had been planted in its place. After the second tree had failed to grow, a third tree was planted which grew at a ferocious pace, doubling its size inside a few short years. It had been planted by Henton Morrow, who had rediscovered the process of producing a form of iron by a particular smelting process. Four years later the tree was dead and, almost to the day, so was the man who had ceremoniously planted it. The medium, who could have had no knowledge of the planter of the tree or his association with metals, said she saw vats with molten metal pouring from them.

As they started to return to the house the medium reported a tunnel was beneath the ground. John knew of the tunnel, but what was known only to very few was that this tunnel was not connected to the present building but to the previous one which had occupied the ground adjacent and at an angle to the modern building. Crossing the tunnel's course she stated she felt an association with the Duke of Marlborough. John Churchill was created Duke of Marlborough following his victory at the Battle of Blenheim – another link to the tree.

Finally they re-entered the building and returned to the reason for them being there, a presence which many staff have reported feeling watching over them. While some mentioned they could sense a presence of the White Lady, the medium disagreed. She said the visitor was a man; he had a military bearing and was wearing a tall and somewhat inelegant hat.

Almost nothing that the medium had reported could have been researched, for nothing has been written down and was previously known to only a very few. Was she tuned in to the events of Bordesley Hall? That decision is left to the individual.

ASTWOOD BANK

Astwood Court

Not one but two ghosts reside at Astwood Court, one of whom is possibly trying to identify themselves.

This house was once the seat of the Culpeper family and, roughly carved into the wainscot is the name of John Culpeper and what may be interpreted as a finger pointing to the floor; tradition has it this points to his final resting place beneath the stone floor of Astwood Court. However, historians insist the family, and particularly John, are recorded as being interred at Hollingbourne in Kent. The ghost of Astwood has, however, often been seen, tripping lightly from the house to the garden and always making for one particular pear tree.

Another ghost has also left her mark. In the earliest days of the nineteenth century a table was moved from where it had stood against a wall for years. This revealed the side of the table where the imprint of a woman's fingers could be seen. It is said this mark was left by the woman after her death when she was already haunting the place. Enraged by her hauntings being completely ignored she struck the table, thus leaving the imprint, and was never seen or heard from again.

We must assume that she was ignored deliberately, for if she was simply not seen or heard how would anyone know when she had given up and left, or even that she had been there in the first place?

White Lion

The White Lion has not one; not two, but at least three and possibly four quite separate apparitions.

Anthony, proprietor of the White Lion, has allowed investigations by a local paranormal group armed with an array of instruments: thermometers to measure temperature range and change, audio equipment to pick up any sounds, cameras to hopefully show what the eyes missed, and lasers to measure dimensions with unerring accuracy. While technology would deal with the physical evidence, experienced psychic investigators employed their own particular skills to detect any presence undetectable by the usual five senses. Their results provided some explanation for what had been witnessed in the 200-year-old former coaching house, said to be the result of 'an angry presence'.

What was once the courtyard and stables for the horse-drawn traffic of the day, has been enclosed and utilised as the function room. By the time the last guest has left after a party or reception here the hour is often late and, quite understandably, some of the clearing up is left until the next morning. However, the following day some of the tables, which the previous night still held glasses and bottles, were clear and everything had been placed neatly on the floor. On another occasion a glass shade on a light had been heard crashing to the floor seconds after someone had left the room. There has also been activity behind the bar. Glasses have fallen from shelves overnight and several members of staff have reported passing through a 'cloud' of intense cold, the feeling was momentary but decidedly real. Even worse was when another glass shade broke away from a light in the area behind the bar, narrowly missing the boss by a matter of inches.

This was not Anthony's first unnerving experience at the White Lion, indeed the first occurred within a week of him taking over the pub. In those days the pub was quite run down, cold and in need of extensive decoration. Undaunted, even relishing the challenge, Anthony went to bed on only the third or fourth night at the pub and soon dropped off to sleep. Throughout his life Anthony's ability to sleep through almost anything is legendary, and in his own words, 'I can sleep at the end of the runway and not be wakened by the jets passing overhead.' So it was somewhat surprising when, at around 3 a.m. that night, he was suddenly awakened by a cold breeze blowing strongly enough to disturb and pass underneath the quilt on the bed. There was no alarm system installed and, fearing someone had left a door or window open (or perhaps worse still there had been a break-in), he rushed downstairs to check. He found no window unlatched, no door unbolted or unlocked and no reason for any movement of air – indeed outside the night was calm and by no means cold.

As he settled into his new home and heard more recollections of the unexplained, Anthony decided to investigate further. He discovered different people were able to detect apparitions, spectres and hauntings by way of the different senses. There were those who saw the image – sight; others reported footsteps and banging – hearing; some felt the cold – touch; and others detected a presence by smell. It is this last olfactory sense which Anthony was particularly interested in because it was relevant to his own experiences. On several occasions he detected the unmistakable aroma of boiled milk, although others standing in the same place could smell nothing. His investigations found a number of reports and recommendations of how to preserve milk in the era before refrigeration by having it boiled – a crude form of pasteurisation.

However, the most unusual story has two chapters, the first shortly after they had settled in and were entertaining friends and relations from their former home town

The White Lion at Astwood Bank.

of Hartlebury. In those days licensing laws regulated the opening hours and, at this time, the gathering was a private one and the doors were closed to the general public until the evening. One young girl needed the toilet but refused to go. Her reluctance was thought to be due to being in an unfamiliar place and the bathroom being a scary large room with its ever-present echoes and plumbing noises. However she insisted she was not scared of the room but of the woman in there and she was well versed in 'the dangers of strangers'. Thus an adult relative accompanied her to ease her worries and, as expected, found the ladies' toilet empty. Reassuring her that there was nobody there she was somewhat unnerved to hear the girl insist there was a woman in there and she even pointed to her – yet she could neither see (nor otherwise sense) anything at all. When they returned to the others the adult told the story out of earshot of the children, but it was soon dismissed as the result of an over-active childhood imagination and forgotten.

By the time of the second chapter of this tale the pub had been decorated and was no longer the gloomy building they had purchased. It was another gathering of friends and family from Hartlebury, this time a different crowd who were celebrating a birthday of one of their number and no children were present. Indeed just about everyone there had passed the 'merry' and 'tipsy' stages when a young (and anonymous) woman, then aged approximately twenty, paid a visit to the same ladies' toilet. Whilst in there she saw a woman walk into and past the stalls, look around her, then leave again. The woman was not particularly old, maybe in her fifties, but seemed 'not all there' having an almost misty appearance. When she returned to the crowd the young woman was visibly shaken and told of what she had just witnessed, refuting suggestions she was so drunk she had imagined it. However, proprietor Anthony and his immediate family recalled the similar story being told by the young girl some months earlier.

It was these earlier events which resulted in the experts being called in to investigate the White Lion At the time of writing only the function room had been examined in detail, so any idea of whom or what has been sensed elsewhere is unknown.

BEOLEY

The Murderer

At the dawn of the nineteenth century a certain house in Beoley was believed to be under the influence of a ghost – said to be the spirit of a murderer who was executed for his crimes some years earlier and who remained here looking for his revenge.

A series of inexplicable events terrified all who stayed here, leading to the house being left empty until something was done to settle the problem. Salvation arrived in the form of the clergy, who met at the house to exorcise the spirit. Banishment could only be achieved by having somewhere to send it. For reasons not readily apparent, the men of the cloth decided to rid themselves of their problem by causing him to be chained to the bed of the Red Sea for a period of fifty years.

It may have rid them of their problem during their lifetimes, yet they either ignored or could not be bothered about the result of their actions after the fifty years were up. Thus half a century later, almost to the day, the ghost returned, determined to exact revenge on anyone he could. The new occupants were subjected to doors slamming, banging on floors and ceilings, and a terrible coldness whenever he passed.

However, he had not reckoned with the tenacity of those now in residence. They set out to chase him from their home. Stamping on floors they tried to drive him through the trapdoor into the cheese room, where they thought he would be trapped.

The Parson

The clergy of Beoley have played an important part in the village's history. So much so that one former holder of the office was apparently reluctant to release his hold on the parish, even in death.

Parson Gittins, who lived in Beoley during the nineteenth century, was troubled. Many unexplained events had befallen him since he had taken up office, not in the church but in the vicarage and he believed that his predecessor's spirit was still in residence. Although nothing dangerous or malicious had so far been encountered, the troubles were becoming a nuisance. Hence the new parson decided to conduct a service to lay his predecessor's spirit to rest. So it was that early one morning the spirit of the clergyman was finally laid to rest, ceremoniously beneath a big tree at the back of the vicarage.

St Leonard's Church in the early winter at Beoley.

BESFORD

The Kennels

At Church Farm, sandwiched between Harewell Lane and the railway line, is the appropriately named Dog Kennel Piece, which accurately recalls its former use.

The kennels in question were those used in the hunt. A hunt's success was dependent on the health, fitness and stamina of the hounds, thus the manor was justifiably proud of its hounds and took great time and trouble to ensure the pack was maintained in peak condition. Hounds were a valuable asset and the skill of the kennelman ensured their value was maintained and even increased by encouraging a good breeding line.

As anyone who has kept dogs will know, a well trained animal will never bark without due reason. Thus when the pack was particularly rowdy and restless one night the master despatched his personal kennelman to seek out the problem. The man never returned and it was not until the following day they realised the awful truth. His body was found ripped to shreds by the very dogs he had cared for so faithfully for so long. Oddly, the only things which had remained untouched were his boots.

On the darkest of nights, when the moon and stars cannot be seen, the sound of ghostly boots can be heard stomping around this same field, while in the distance the unmistakable sound of howling hounds is a chilling reminder of that night.

Dower House

One of the strangest and most recent hauntings in Worcestershire is based around Dower House. There have been four different manifestations here, which may be the same individual seen from differing aspects.

Inside the house a mist slowly formed itself into the shape of a woman before dissipating, and a woman has been seen on several occasions looking into the same room through the window; again she fades from view. Intensely bright lights have also been witnessed shining into the room, although there is no source for these lights.

The most interesting phenomenon has been seen outside. Two witnesses stood and watched in astonishment as a light shone on an outside wall, again without any discernable light source. Furthermore, while they cast no shadows on the wall, they watched in astonishment as the shadow of a person was seen to cross the wall without anyone or anything there to cast it.

Besford Court

Less than a kilometre north-east of Church Farm is Besford Court. Today it is a school, however this manor house has been standing here for some time and has seen significant changes in the village and also appears to have acquired a spirit or two along the way.

An upstairs bedroom is the most popular location for the ghost – or possibly ghosts – to appear. Sometimes the apparition is said to resemble a nun, however there is no known historical tie to a convent or any religious establishment. Therefore perhaps the figure has been seen indistinctly and is instead a lady in grey, which has also been seen here.

BEWDLEY

Running Horse

The Running Horse public house is a picturesque listed building standing on the road known as Long Bank, which runs down from Callow Hill to Bewdley and across the River Severn. Folklore tells how Welsh raiders would chase the English down the hill and across the river, pausing to enjoy a flagon of ale in the Running Horse. It seems the Welsh were prepared to infiltrate English territory by a considerable distance in order to find a refreshing brew.

The Running Horse is a charming establishment, with open fireplaces, traditional decor, and many nooks and crannies for those who prefer a little privacy. On my visit staff served up an excellent meal which was washed down with a pint of real ale and tales of two ghosts.

The first is a slim young lady with long hair, and attire which can only have come from the 1970s. She mostly appears just as the establishment is closing, when only staff and maybe a very few customers are left. Nobody has any idea of who she might be, or why

Running Horse, Bewdley.

she needs to haunt the pub. She does not speak or interact with anyone, simply walking through the room and disappearing around a corner. Indeed she seems completely oblivious of anyone else being present, which is the only thing she has in common with the second visitor from the past.

In the inter-war years the pub offered much the same as it does today, a fine selection of ales and an excellent menu, and a man was employed here to prepare the meals for patrons. However, one day, after the pub was closed to the public, the chef committed suicide in the pub kitchens. His ghost has been seen wandering around behind the scenes late at night, although his presence is more often revealed by the sound of pots, pans and utensils being dropped or thrown around.

Woodcolliers

The Woodcolliers pub almost appears to be carved into the side of the hill overlooking Bewdley. It was never created as a single building, being an amalgamation of four or possibly five former houses. This gives the interior the feeling of a maze, with cosy little nooks and crannies around every corner. Another attraction is the beer which, as I was reliably informed by a kindly gent who pointed the author in the right direction of the pub, is the finest in the town.

The present owners, Roger and Anna, moved in just over two years ago. Although today the spirits appear to have accepted the new arrivals, this was not so when they first arrived and there was an amazing amount of activity. One of the first things they noticed was an overwhelming sense of a primitive consciousness. So persistent was this presence that they checked on previous licensees and found one who was described as an 'idiot', used as a medical term rather than an insult, who resided in the pub for a substantial period of time.

Upstairs is a small area which has been used as a utility or laundry room. Reached via a series of short stairs, there have been times when the lady of the house has heard footsteps following her on these stairs. However, they cannot have been echoes of her own steps for they were much faster, as if someone was running.

The laundry room had a surprise in store one day. Noticing the light had been left on in the middle of the day, Anna went to switch it off and found the switch had been in the 'off' position all the time, even though the light was on. Such electrical problems were not restricted to upstairs. Down in the bar one afternoon a former landlord watched the switch for the lights turning itself on and off, and the lights responding, yet there was nobody within reach.

As it is a collection of properties, several rooms have been utilised as the cellar over time. One door, which was clearly once an exit route, now leads to a cellar. The cellar is no longer used and the previous tenant's daughter refused to enter, so oppressive did she find the atmosphere. Another cellar, now blocked off, lies underneath the centre room. When they first moved in, Roger and Anna and several customers reported sensing that they were close to the site of an accident. They felt that a man was lying injured, awaiting a rescue which only came after he had endured much suffering. No record or

The Woodcolliers at Bewdley.

memory of such an accident has yet been uncovered. The current cellar has one small nook where the wine is kept and, while the rest of the cellar is now at peace, this small area has produced a feeling of panic on several occasions.

Back upstairs in the main bar four regular customers and a staff member were seated in the public area one evening. It was early and the five individuals who knew each other very well indeed were engaged in the friendly banter so often heard in a pub. Without warning four large-stemmed wine glasses, which were stored upside-down in the slots over the bar, slid back out for no reason whatsoever and smashed onto the floor. What was even more disconcerting was they had come from different areas, while other glasses more precariously stored remained safe and sound.

However, the most unsettling event happened about ten years ago. A long-time regular customer was sitting in the room where the log fire burned. He was suddenly aware of an old man sitting in the corner a short way along the same seat. Being a polite and friendly gentleman he spoke. Yet when he received no reply and the old gent did not acknowledge him he became concerned and reached out to see if the man was in need of assistance. Imagine his surprise when he found his hand pass straight through the old man!

The poor man was so shocked that he ran into the next room with his beer, downed it in one and, after telling what had happened, swore he would never return to the Woodcolliers ever again. To this day he has never returned.

No identities have been suggested for these ghostly individuals, save for the former landlord. However, they now seem to have accepted the new arrivals and the owners are looking forward to a pleasant co-existence, at least for the time being.

Horn & Trumpet

While the first record of a named landlord here dates from 1845, the Horn & Trumpet is certainly older than this. There have been several strange events at this hostelry, mainly in the public area downstairs.

The place has long offered an overnight bed to the weary. One evening, when nobody was in residence upstairs – not management, staff, nor guests – doors were heard slamming as if someone were systematically searching every room. On examination the upstairs was found to be completely empty, there was no sign that anyone had been there, and everywhere was secure.

Downstairs in the bars there have been more reports of activity. A dog walked in one evening accompanied by its master. Quite out of character the animal refused to settle, shied away, was clearly terrified of something and wanted nothing more than to leave the place without delay. Eventually the man was forced to down his newly-purchased drink and take the dog home. A few months after this, when the bar was occupied by about a dozen customers, menus had been placed along the bar in the hope of tempting the customers to partake of the excellent menu. Suddenly, and without a hint of a breeze, these menus were swept from the bar and onto the bar room floor.

The Horn & Trumpet, Bewdley.

However, the most unusual occurrence was reported by the male customers. It was only men who encountered the problem for it happened within that exclusively male domain – the gents' toilet. On more occasions than can be remembered, as they passed through the door hands were felt pushing from behind in order to hasten their progress through it. Fortunately, the invisible occupant was thoughtful enough only to push them out after they had availed themselves of the facilities.

Pack Horse

The Pack Horse was originally a carrier's pub and a clearing house for goods in transit and dates from at least the fifteenth century. Before the canals, the railways and road transport, there were just two ways to move goods: along the navigable rivers, or over land by horsepower. Neither of these methods were ideal – navigable rivers served little of the area of the country, although most major settlements grew up on these watercourses, and the roads were not made to carry heavy carts. Hence the vast majority of the miles were covered by teams of pack horses. Work animals loaded with grain, cloth, minerals, meats and anything which could be traded were moved to and from the quays and docks to points along the route for distribution within the local area. The local inn was the most obvious place to act as the distribution centre – it was already a major meeting point, it provided hostelry for the travellers, while many had their own blacksmith adjacent to the inn. Furthermore the pub would naturally have more storage room which could be utilised.

From 1818 the Pack Horse, with a much better transportation system now in place, predominantly acted as an inn and hostelry and James Lane was the first landlord. By 1840 Bewdley had two claims to fame: it had the highest concentration of licensed premises compared to population in the whole of England, which probably contributed somewhat to its other claim – the highest crime rate in Worcestershire. Back at the Pack Horse there was one legal loophole which was readily exploited – a long-standing law on the books meant licensing hours were regulated by the clientele, specifically that as long as there was a bed empty the pub could remain open for business!

When speaking to Mark, the current landlord, he was unaware of any reports of the unexplained at the pub and suggested speaking to one or two of the long-time regulars. This was excellent advice and paid dividends within minutes with a tale which fits with Bewdley's boisterous reputation from the nineteenth century.

It was late at night after a busy evening and in the bar two staff members were wearily cleaning glasses and tidying away bottles. Suddenly they were aware of sounds of angry voices and what sounded like fighting outside the pub. Before calling the police they looked out to make sure the sounds were outside their own pub and that the police were not already on the scene. However, they were stunned to find there was no mob, no fight, nothing untoward whatsoever, just the usual late-night passers-by heading for home in a steady shower of rain. Had they heard an echo of the mid-nineteenth century, a reminder of a street brawl?

As far as anyone knew this ghostly fight had never been heard before or since, yet there were other examples of a similar nature. In the early morning, when just the cleaning staff were in the public area, a loud knock summoned them to the door. However, when it was opened there was nobody there. On another occasion staff heard a dog barking fitfully, seemingly trapped in the private area at the rear of the building, and yet there was no dog living on the premises at that time. Fearing an intruder, thinking perhaps the animal had been somehow trapped, they investigated but the moment they opened the door the sounds stopped and the area was found to be empty.

On another occasion the sound of a well-shod horse crossing the cobbles could be heard; possibly an echo from the days when the place was effectively a distribution centre. The sounds were heard with such clarity that even the occasional slip of the metal shoe could be made out. As the spectral horse departed the area it quickened its gait a little and faded into the distance. Those present at the time were said to have been left speechless for several moments afterwards.

Oddly the majority of the reports have come from outside the pub itself. However, there have been several individuals who have reported feeling an unusual sensation inside the premises. It seems to be in the narrowest passages, doorways, and in the tightest corners this is felt, in doorways, bottlenecks, and in the cellars someone has been felt brushing past and seems to be in something of a hurry. This is a particularly rare event when it comes to ghost stories, for a sense of urgency is rarely commented upon.

It was interesting to listen to the reports, albeit these were second, third or even fourth hand narratives. Furthermore, it should be noted that the reports outside the Pack Horse cannot conclusively be said to be associated with the pub itself, particularly that of the brawl.

BREDON

The Black Dog

In England it is known variously as Black Shuck, Bogey Beast, Bargeheust, Capelthwaite, Gallytrot, Guytrash, Gurt Dog, Padfoot or Skriker; in Scotland Cu Sith or Mauthe Doog; and in Ireland Pooka; whatever the name, the terror of facing the black dog every bit as fearsome as that created by Arthur Conan Doyle in *The Hound of the Baskervilles* is the same.

During one of the balmy summer evenings of the Second World War, a great beast paid a visit to a cottage in the village of Bredon. As with other families throughout the land the men folk were away serving King and country, leaving the women and children at home.

A young girl had been sent to bed, it was past her bedtime, yet she was far from sleepy. The war, with all its many dangers, seemed a distant threat and her mind was reliving the delights of her idyllic day in the sun. Sitting on the end of the big bed, her fingers were idly toying with the ornamental knobs of the brass bedstead as she gazed out of the open window. Below she could hear the sounds of her mother and aunt in conversation and, in the distance, the familiar bell of the van and the promise of a fried fish supper.

It was then she heard a scratching sound. Turning, she saw a huge black dog padding slowly across the room. It appeared to have emerged from the empty hearth and was walking around the corner of the bed and passed directly between it and the window. Suddenly it swivelled its head around to stare directly at the girl. It had blood red eyes which seemed to glow from within the very skull of the beast. She was conscious of its hot breath, like a gust of wind on her skin. Despite being as high up as she was, seated upon that great bed, that awful dog's eyes were level with hers. It continued to stare at her until it reached the door, where it promptly vanished.

She sat for a long time afterwards, too scared to move. Although that was many years ago, the details have remained as sharp as ever and will remain with her always.

Refurbished Cottages

Often a change to a building or those that live there can prove the catalyst for ghostly activity. In the village of Bredon, overlooked by the better known hill of the same name, a number of cottages were bought and had been converted in order to provide modern housing. Three quite distinct reports later came from these properties.

First footsteps were heard crossing an upstairs floor; however this wooden flooring had been removed as part of the refurbishment. It was also reported that an elderly man had entered one bedroom and woken the person sleeping there. Later an aroma was detected in another building, said to be reminiscent of the collective perfume of the many flowers found at a funeral. The scent was particularly strong around the area by a doorway, however when this was later replaced by a window the scent was never detected again. Finally the vague outline of a figure accompanied by its shadow was seen passing in front of the white wall of the cottage but disappeared when it reached the corner of the building.

BRETFORTON

St Leonard's Church

Many places the size of Bretforton, which in the early twenty-first century has a population of under 1,000, would expect one or maybe two ghosts at most. However, in and around the churchyard at Bretforton more ghosts have been reportedly seen than can be counted on two hands.

St Leonard's Church at Bretforton.

Across the main road from the church is the manor house and these two major buildings in the village have both been the haunt of a medieval monk. The man of the cloth does not interact, nor does he seem to notice the existence of anyone else, but simply continues slowly and steadily on toward wherever he is heading.

Also seen around here is the headless woman. Just who she is and why she is headless are unknown. Yet she seems to portray the role perfectly, the head tucked in the traditional position in the crook of the arm.

The rest of the sightings have centred on the churchyard itself. Indeed they are all seen together. Dressed in what has been described as typical eighteenth-century attire, the number in the funeral procession is uncertain but is certainly well into double figures. Whose funeral this represents is unknown, yet sightings have been reported over more than a century.

Vanished Trackway

Those of the spirit world appear to have a greater knowledge of the ancient pathways of our world than any archaeologist or map. Over the years there have been many reports of a coach and horses following a road which takes it through hedges, across fields and over ditches, seemingly following a road which no longer exists between Bretforton and the Littletons. Any remaining thoughts this may be a real coach and horses are dispelled when we realise the hooves of the horses and the wheels of the coach leave no tracks, while on closer inspection the coachman urging the animals on has no head.

Fleece Inn

The Fleece Inn is among the most picturesque of public houses to be found anywhere in the land. Built in around 1400 by a farming family named Byrd, this longhouse was constructed to house both the family and livestock, as was quite normal for the day.

The property remained a part of the farm until it was rebuilt in the nineteenth century as a pub. Henry Byrd, a direct descendant of the original yeoman farmer, obtained a license to sell ale and cider in 1848. Indeed both brews were produced on site for almost 100 years. Eventually the pub came to Henry's great-granddaughter, Lola Taplin, in 1947, and she ran it single-handed for thirty years until her death at the age of eighty-three. In her will she left the property to the National Trust, with the proviso that it should continue to be run as it had been for over a century and remain an unspoilt traditional English country pub.

As much a working museum as a pub, the three principal rooms contain items which would otherwise likely have been lost. The Brewhouse still has the wooden malt shovel on the wall, while the harvest barrels hanging from the ceiling beam were used to provide cider for the workers in the fields at harvest time. This room's collection is topped off with Victorian measuring containers, in brass and copper, which are stamped to show authenticity.

In the Pewter Room there is an impressive collection of pewter which, if legends are to be believed, was left by Oliver Cromwell in exchange for gold and silver with which he paid the Parliamentary armies. This was originally the farm's kitchen and roasting spits and pans are left hanging over the grate.

The final room is the Dugout, which was once the farmhouse pantry. A coffin-like table with a hinged lid provided a place to store dough to allow it to rise before being baked in the bread oven. In the grounds a large round stone, once a part of the cider press, is flanked by smaller mushroom-like straddle stones. These straddles supported the wooden platforms upon which the grain was stored, the specially worked overhangs prevented rodents and other pests from raiding the valuable grain.

Inside the pub the original worn flagstones, log fires and solid wooden beams give a feeling of the age of the place, while much of the furniture from the original home is still utilised as a part of the decor. Lola Taplin hung charms above the entry points of doors and windows, while the joints between the flagstones around every hearth were marked by the traditional chalk circles to deter witches and demons from entering the building via the chimney.

Ever since the National Trust took over the running of the property in 1977 the pub has been subjected to inexplicable events. Food and other objects are said to be thrown around the bar. Lola is cited as the culprit; she has returned to keep an eye on her beloved pub and presumably sometimes finds things which displease her. Indeed

The Fleece Inn, Bretforton.

there seems to be no pattern to her displeasure, except perhaps untidiness. On one occasion, with four individuals in the pub who were all quite sober as it was still early in the morning, a saucer left on top of the coffee machine was the target for Lola's irritation. The witnesses watched as the saucer flew across the room; it did not drop or fall, but had a trajectory as if thrown. This has also been the case with pictures on the walls which appear to have been thrown – perhaps she was unimpressed by these images.

Maybe Lola was trying to warn of what was to come, for in February 2004 the 700-year-old building suffered a disastrous fire after the thatch caught light. The damage was extensive, yet could have been much worse had it occurred at night. Thanks to the rapid response of the emergency services most of the damage was confined to the upper floor and the irreplaceable furniture and items were saved. Indeed most of the damage to the lower floor was done by the hoses used to extinguish the flames. The doors at the back of the dugout were guarded by a line of Lola's old shoes. Normally movind them to use the doors incurred her displeasure, but she appears to have called an amnesty during the fire to allow the fireman to fling open the doors and even move the shoes.

Expert restoration workers were called in and Bretforton saw a grand re-opening of the Fleece Inn in 2005. Nothing has been heard from Lola since, so perhaps her actions were a warning, does she simply approves of the new modifications to the kitchen and lavatories?

Such psychic activity has attracted the attention of many claiming to be tuned in to this phenomena. In a corner of the Pewter Room on more than one occasion visitors have reported seeing men seated at a small rectangular table enjoying an ale and in quiet conversation. The similarities in these reports which, as far as is known, have never been recorded previously is surprising. Each is said to be wearing the brown coarse clothing of labourers, were hatted, and one is smoking a clay pipe – a quintessentially English rural scene from the eighteenth century. These men pay no heed to the other customers and, in these days of a smoke-free environment in Britain's pubs, no reports of the smell of burning pipe tobacco. Often aromas and sensations are all that most receive from their ghostly visitors and yet in this instance the reverse seems to be true; a case of being seen and not heard, nor felt or indeed even smelled. In fact the only discrepancies in these quite separate reports is the numbers involved, for some say three men and others quote four. Maybe the difference is down to one of the number paying a visit to the privy.

Well of Sadness

Bretforton's reputation as 'the most haunted village in Worcestershire' is a statement based on the ratio between the number of ghosts and permanent residents. Anyone who has visited this delightful corner of the county will not be surprised to find how many remain here long after their lives have ended. One such individual appears to be happier here as a visitor from the afterlife than she ever had been in the physical world.

The actual date of her death is masked in a veil of myth and mystery, indeed there seems to be no official record of her death at all. This is not surprising as the woman committed suicide, thus she was denied a burial on consecrated ground. Until 1837 church records were the sole method of recording births, deaths and marriages and had done so for exactly 300 years, while prior to this the church records were voluntary and not a legal requirement. Hence it is only in the last two centuries that we have anything like a complete record of what have become known colloquially as 'hatches, matches and despatches'.

Little is known of the life of Spot Loggins, apart from the circumstances surrounding her death. Her misery was certain, for she took her own life as a result of that age-old tale of unrequited love, however, we have no idea who the object of her affections was, nor is there any suggestion which would help to provide a date. This may be a clue to the identity of the lover, for it would probably take someone in power to throw a blanket of secrecy over the tale, which thus suggests a family member of the lords of the manor, the landed gentry, or perhaps even the clergy.

The object of her affections will never be known, but the result is. Behind the church a quiet country lane leads across the brook and to a public footpath. It is here we find the well into which Spot Loggins is said to have hurled herself in her grief and was drowned. Today the 'well' is little more than a couple of loose rocks laid over a minimal crevice in the earth, yet this is not unexpected, for wells will silt up fairly quickly when not in use. Despite the image of a round bricked wall lining a well which dramatists have depicted, this is anything but true for most wells which

Spot Loggins' Well, hidden in the undergrowth.

were kept open through use alone. Sodden earth would soon fall from the sides and be trapped as it became overgrown and rather quicker than one would think would well-nigh fill the gap entirely. Of course the water of the spring would still be flowing, thus the channel would remain open below ground through natural erosion. Thus it is difficult to know what kind of well poor Spot Loggins threw herself into, for it seems equally plausible that she became wedged in a tight-fitting hole and asphyxiated rather than drowned.

Many suicides who were not laid to rest in consecrated ground are reputed to haunt the region where they were buried. A favourite spot for such burials was at crossroads, where the lack of obvious direction was designed to confuse the restless spirit and imprison it. However, this does not seem to have been the case here and other methods have been employed to appease Spot Loggins' spirit. On the third Wednesday of November each year, a band of hardy locals and interested visitors visit the well to sing a song or two and say a prayer to bless the memory of the woman. It is hoped that this annual pilgrimage to the place of her death will appease her tortured spirit for another year.

As has been noted, any idea of the date of her death, birth or anything about her is lost in antiquity. This date in November has been chosen arbitrarily to fill a void between the summer and Christmas and, as one member of the community confided, 'It also coincides with early closing day for the local shops.'

BROADWAY

Ephraim Rolfe

During the eighteenth century Broadway was home to one Ephraim Rolfe. A popular young man, he was known to be a little slow-witted. Yet he was famous around here for his kindness to the local children and an uncanny ability to seemingly communicate with animals. Indeed he even managed to earn a pittance of a salary scaring birds from the local fields and thus help protect the crops.

One day he was out patrolling the land in and around Springfield Lane to the north of the village heading in the general direction of Evesham. He was spotted by the squire and, thinking he had finally caught the poacher who had plagued him for years, took aim and shot him dead.

It is said that Ephraim still lingers around the fields where he met his sad and premature end. On stormy nights, when brief illumination is provided by lightning or moonlight between the clouds, he can be glimpsed – scarecrow thin and bony, still protecting the crops around the village where he was loved.

Middle Hill Wood

Not every ghostly occurrence features a human being, or indeed necessarily a former life-form. However, it is difficult to see how any inanimate object can suddenly acquire the ability to move of its own volition. For example if a glass or ornament flies across the room it is considered to have been thrown by a ghost and not to have leapt all on its own.

Such a phenomenon is seen, or actually heard, in Middle Hill Wood 2km south of Broadway. During the Dissolution of the Monasteries it was common practice for the clergy to hide as many of their valuables as they thought they could get away with. This did not always mean gold and silver, and in this case the bells of the church, a costly item to replace and a certain target for destruction by the King's forces, were hidden in among the trees to be retrieved at a later date. However, few people knew their whereabouts and their location was forgotten.

Four centuries later the British nation was fighting a world war for the second time in just twenty-five years. During the war years the ringing of church bells for religious purposes was prohibited by law. The locals were therefore stunned when they heard the sound of bells coming from the woods. Bells were only to be rung to signal an invasion, thus the people were justifiably scared by the sound. When they later realised it was nothing to do with an invasion they were angered by the act.

They soon realised where the sound was coming from and wondered how such heavy objects could be rung without a great deal of preparatory work. Church bells are solid castings of metal and even the smallest are extraordinarily heavy and too much for any one individual to carry. Then they realised that what they were hearing were the missing church bells and that whomever was sounding these peals was likely not of this world.

BROMSGROVE

Avoncroft Museum

South of Bromsgrove, near the island on the A38, is a museum with a difference – the Avoncroft Museum. Not content just to keep furniture, clothing and other household items of historical interest, this museum has taken to displaying whole buildings!

As with so many old properties, there had been the normal reports of the unusual happenings and the intrigued staff organised a séance. So it was that a dozen brave individuals, two experts and members of staff, settled down to an all-nighter. The usual assortment of temperature gauges, cameras and tape recorders were in evidence, and also the old favourite – the ouija board.

Each member of the group had brought a list of every report they had heard since they were associated with the place and, as there were some long-serving members of staff present, this produced a good few years experience to the meeting. It came as a surprise to all just how many unexplained events there had been at the museum. Remember, all these events have occurred at the museum itself and not at the buildings on the original sites.

An old forge stands alongside what has been used for the main office building. On one occasion a member of staff witnessed people walking past the window. Those walking past were not wearing clothes from the present day, but their attire seemed to place them in the eighteenth century or earlier. Their dress would suggest they were workers associated with the forge, such as blacksmiths or farriers. Around this time the sound of chimes was reported by one person, although on reflection it seems the noise was closer to that of a hammer hitting an anvil.

In the same building an office worker had the feeling of someone constantly looking over her shoulder. For reasons she was unable to explain, she knew the person was an old accountant checking to see how the work was progressing. Eventually she became so frustrated that she told him, 'Go, the work is done!' after which the feeling evaporated.

In the toll house, where various items are displayed, several members of staff had locked the building at night only to open up the following morning and find several pieces had been moved. None of the items were ever missing and they had not been moved far. Indeed it seemed almost as if the items had been picked up, examined, and put down without thought as to where they had come from.

During an inspection of the various buildings one psychic investigator felt extremely claustrophobic in the big hall, as if there was no way out, and was not surprised to find the windows of the original building had never been replaced.

One of the strangest stories involved a member of the public. A twelve-year-old girl had arrived with her family and was touring the site. As she exited one of the buildings she felt someone thump her quite hard on the back, yet nobody was behind her nor anywhere near her and the building was empty. She soon reported she was suffering great discomfort from the area where she had been hit and an examination showed a vivid red mark had appeared.

Back at the séance the ouija board was brought out. The organisers performed a series of tests to show there was no possible trickery involved in moving the glass. When all were certain there was no foul play the experiment commenced. Several members of the meeting were visibly shaken when the glass correctly wished one of those present 'Happy Birthday'. During the test the psychic investigators recorded a number of drops in temperature in the room, while the table tipped at strange angles several times for no apparent reason.

However, the most intriguing story concerns one member of staff. This sad tale began some years ago when she was a young girl of five or six. At this time she had a friend called Angela with whom she played almost every day. The girls had become firm friends and so it was a great loss when Angela suddenly stopped coming around and she was no longer taken to play at her friend's house. Every time she asked where Angela was, nobody would give her a clear answer.

At the séance a girl came through and asked that her former friend should let her go, so she could find eternal rest. The girl's name was Angela. Next opportunity she had the member of staff who remembered her young friend called her mother and asked, once again, what had happened to her friend all those years ago. It was with great sadness that her mother told her how they had hidden the awful truth from their daughter. Angela had been unable to play again because she had died, murdered by her own father.

The staff member was told that, now she was aware of the facts, Angela would be able to find rest as all the loose ends had now been tied up. Since that time nobody has been aware of Angela's presence.

Golden Cross

The Golden Cross Hotel in the high street was previously known as the Black Monk. During this period it was run by a management duo who did not live on the premises. One night at 4 a.m. they were both called out from their respective homes by the police as they were the nominated key holders and the burglar alarm had reported an illegal entry to the building.

They arrived to find the local constabulary already on the scene and no sign of any forced entry. As a matter of procedure they were asked to open the building so the police could check that nothing was amiss within. A thorough and meticulous search of the entire building was conducted and, when nothing was found, it was assumed the alarm had sounded in error and they left the managers to lock up again. Every door and lock had been opened and it took some time to lock up again, but eventually the

Ghostly children were heard playing outside the Golden Cross Hotel at Bromsgrove.

two met up in the remaining room. It was then that one of the owners pointed out a reflection in a large mirror in the bar to his colleague.

She looked to see a scene which was not visible within the pub. In the mirror she saw a number of children in Victorian clothing playing happily, yet the room around her was empty save for the two key holders.

F. W. Woolworth

The former Woolworth's building in Bromsgrove is contained within the shells of former houses in the High Street. These houses were built over a century ago and have seen much of the modern history of the town.

One particular spirit was thought to haunt the stock rooms during the 1980s. The boy, who came to be known as Charlie, was said to have sat at this window during his lifetime. One of the few great pleasures in his life was watching the children play from this window, for he had had polio and as a result was unable to join them.

Whenever anyone left boxes in front of this window overnight, thus blocking the view, they were found knocked to the floor the next morning.

The upstairs window where the young ghost's activity was discerned.

Ye Olde Black Cross

Ye Olde Black Cross pub was here during the time of the English Civil War and, in particular, the Battle of Worcester. It is named such because it stands at a crossroads, a place where executed criminals and alleged witches were buried to prevent their spirits from finding eternal rest in consecrated ground.

The place is said to be the haunt of a Royalist soldier and supporter of the King, whom he is reputed to still be seeking. It is part of folklore that Charles II, escaping the final battle of the Civil War, stopped here to have the shoes of his horse replaced by the blacksmith who worked the forge to the rear of the premises.

BROMYARD

Falcon Hotel

The Falcon Hotel dates from the middle of the sixteenth century. This Tudor black and white half-timbered construction still exhibits a medieval fireplace, ornate plaster ceiling and oak-panelled walls. During the eighteenth century the ballroom block was built and the building virtually doubled in size.

The old stable block was a busy place in Victorian times, with a hay loft, resident ostler and room for sixty animals, and was later utilised as a garage. In February 1947 the local cinema was closed when a heavy snowfall brought about the collapse of the corrugated roof of the cinema. The ballroom of the Falcon was pressed into use as an emergency cinema. It continued to be so utilized until the new cinema was completed on the site of the garage.

This post-Second World War era is relevant, for the clothing of the gentleman said to wander the second floor points to the latter years of the 1940s. The young man in question, smartly suited and complete with collar and tie, is said to enquire of those he meets, 'Where is Anne?' before moving on, apparently continuing his search.

Some reports state he is 'not all there', although whether this is questioning if he is completely solid or commenting on his sanity is unknown.

CALLOW END

Prior's Court

No less than four quite distinct ghosts have been reported at Prior's Court, which was built in Elizabethan times upon the site of a thirteenth-century priory; the ghostly quartet range in age from the days of the priory itself, right up to the Victorian era.

The longest resident is a woman. According to legend, she hurried to the priory to take shelter during a particularly severe storm. Whilst it may have seemed a place of safety, it is maintained she was raped and subsequently murdered by the monks. Her body was disposed of in the depths of the nearby River Severn. Her screams are still heard echoing through the night sky during breaks in the storm and her ghost has also been seen running through the lanes around here.

Within the confines of the house a Cavalier has been seen wandering the rooms. His identity is a mystery; however the circumstances of his death may have been uncovered. During restoration work the skeleton and clothing of a man, a Royalist, were found interred in a chimney. The man had almost certainly been hiding here, possibly following his escape from the Battle of Naseby.

The most recent addition to the corridors is the ghost of a young Victorian girl. She is in her teens, sometimes wears a straw hat or may be seen carrying it revealing her long hair pinned up in a bun. In recent times she has been seen wandering outside, seemingly enjoying a leisurely walk between the courtyard and the orchard.

The last entity appears in the bedroom. Described as a strangely shaped visitation, it has no recognisable form. Being unknown may be a contributory factor in seeing it as malevolent, although none have reported having suffered any harm – at least not so far.

Prior's Court Revisited

In the 1950s media attention turned to Prior's Court. However, this was not a ghost story in a form ever encountered by the author which is why it is dealt with separately.

The lady of the house had apparently been trying for some time to hire domestic staff, essential for a residence of this size. One couple, who had been offered the positions which meant living in, had accepted and were keen to begin until they visited the village and heard of the unseen residents of Prior's Court. They refused to stay another moment. This was one of the examples cited when speaking at a tribunal in Upton-upon-Severn, where she was claiming a rate reduction because of her non-paying guests.

She claimed everything possible had been done to solve the problem, indeed one spirit had successfully been exorcised in 1906. She had never seen a ghost personally but had certainly sensed their presence. No end to the problem could be seen as nobody would stay in the house after nightfall, not once the villagers learned where any newcomers were staying.

Amazingly she won her case and the annual rateable value was reduced by £8 to £105. However, records tend to suggest this may have been more to do with the water supply. There were no water mains to the house, all water being drawn from a well which, when analysed, was found to be most unsuitable for consumption.

A reduction of 7 per cent is paltry compensation for a lack of clean water, but an excellent result if the claim was awarded for spectral dependants.

CHURCH LENCH

An Awful Abode

For many years in the early nineteenth century locals were aware of a house in the village being the headquarters for organised crime. A band of ruffians were to be found within these walls, a collection of the foulest felons, thieves, footpads and murderers.

To speak of it was to invite retribution, and none of the residents of Church Lench wanted that kind of trouble. Indeed a servant in the village, who had dared to threaten to reveal their evil deeds, promptly disappeared and was never heard from again.

Eventually after many, many years the gang dispersed, leaving the building empty. Part of it was pulled down to provide room for the school, the remaining building offered for rent. The demolition work had uncovered human bones beneath the floor, even in the very foundations themselves. When the news broke regarding the skeletal remains it served only to fuel the rumours of the haunted house.

Tenants were hard to find, even those who refused to accept the existence of any ghosts. Outsiders, who knew nothing of the history of the place, were reluctant to remain here. The place was said to be cold and oppressive. Bumps and screams were heard regularly, loud noises were heard coming from upstairs, as though large and heavy objects had fallen and rolled across the upstairs floor. Yet on inspection nothing was found to have been disturbed.

Some saw strange glowing lights on the walls. Yet worse still was the tormented figure seen to float through several of the rooms carrying a candle. While there is a flickering light emanating from the flame of the candle, the light does not cast the shadow of anything from this world.

CLAINES

The Mug House

The Mug House at Claines is an old inn with a history dating back at least nine centuries. A timber-framed building it has undergone refurbishment many times but retains its original character.

Originally a brew house for the church, it is unique in being the only premises in the country to stand on consecrated ground licensed to sell alcohol. All brew houses owned by the Church were closed in the seventeenth century, for puritans frowned upon the drunken revellers' lewd behaviour.

A great storm in the twentieth century damaged an outer wall part of which had to be reconstructed. When the repairs were being carried out, a bishop's crozier was found within the wall itself. It was identified as belonging to the Bishops of Worcester, and today it resides in Claines Church of St John the Baptist. How it got in the wall, or why, is a complete mystery.

The unusual circumstances surrounding the crozier are not blamed for the ghostly occurrences within the Mug House itself. Doors routinely open and close entirely of their own volition, for no apparent reason. Within the cellar are tools used solely to open new barrels, and these have been known to be moved about, which is somewhat inconvenient when a new barrel is needed at the busiest times. It was here that a keg of cider was drawn across the floor in full view of a witness who was seemingly alone there. At another time a 'nine of mild', one of the real ales kept on a specially constructed trestle along each side of the cellar, and was still hooked up to the taps upstairs, had been moved across to the middle of the cellar. Another time six five-litre bottles of cleaning fluid (used to ensure the pipes are kept spotless) were being placed in a storage space created especially for this purpose. A small recess below a table will take the six containers in two rows of three. As one can image, five litres of fluid is not the easiest thing to move into such a small space. Thus by the time the back three were in place and the last of the front row was neatly placed in the recess it was somewhat unnerving to see it slide back out 6in or so. Furthermore this happened a second and yet a third time before the playful ghost was severely rebuked for wasting valuable time!

The stories of the ghosts of the Mug House reached the ears of one group who asked for the chance to allow twenty or so older teenagers the opportunity to spend the night in a haunted cellar. Reluctantly Judy, agreed on the provision that they obey certain rules.

The Mug House: the only pub in England to stand on consecrated ground.

Firstly they should not touch the beer and second, owing to the fact the room would be in total darkness, they should take to their sleeping bags and not move around as it would be decidedly dangerous to do so. Of course her worries were justifiable for both rules had clearly been broken by 4 a.m. She was forced to open the door to the cellar and yell above the hubbub issuing from within, 'What's going on in there?' After that the noise did diminish, yet the next day it seems she had not heard the same as others who were staying at the pub that night. It seems other guests at the pub had heard the unmistakable mechanical sound of a jack-in-the-box playing. Indeed they had misunderstood Judy's admonishing of the noisy teenagers as her having heard the musical child's toy. It later transpired that a few of those in the cellar had heard the same thing but had been too scared by the ridicule of their peers to report it.

Another strange occurrence happened one day when Judy was looking across at the clock on the wall. It was a ship's clock and suddenly the glass face, which had been bolted on, popped off and flew across the room. The clock had stopped at precisely 2.15 in the afternoon. A few weeks later she was relating the story to a customer in another room and took them to see the timepiece which was still hanging on the wall. Judy was amazed to find the clock was working again and, moreover, was showing the correct time.

Pictures and other items have also been known to be thrown from the walls. A notable event occurred one Sunday when the pub was closed and friends had been invited to a barbecue at this idyllic location. However, true to the tradition of a British outdoor event, the rain forced the guests indoors. They had not been inside for more than twenty minutes when a shelf of glasses fell behind the bar, just the drinking vessels fell; the shelf itself stayed where it had always been and was firmly fixed. What was even more surprising was the state of the glassware there. There was not a large piece of glass remaining as would normally be expected; instead the glass appeared to had been ground into a scattering of minute fragments and slivers.

In other parts of the pub, particularly upstairs in the living quarters, there is a feeling of not being alone, of a presence. In the kitchen in 2008 Judy had felt a tug on her hair, yet there was nobody behind her and nothing to snag her hair on. Furthermore the snug, often thought to be the most active place after the cellar, has one corner which seems to be off limits to dogs. Many dogs which entered the snug would not settle, kept staring into the corner and whimpering, while a family pet refused to enter the room altogether.

To some there is no doubt this is all the work of the pub's resident ghost, Bert. A resident of Claines until his death in the 1940s, Bert was a regular in the pub. Despite his wealth he was not liked, being a particularly unpleasant individual. Indeed one contemporary landlord was once heard to tell Bert he was such a miserable individual that, were he a ghost, he would be too mean to bother to attempt to haunt anyone or anywhere. It seems this seemingly innocent comment by former landlord Wally Trow has resulted in Bert having a change of heart. As a ghost Bert can certainly be bothered to haunt the pub where he spent much of his time.

Yet Judy believes the ghost is unlikely to be that of Bert; Bert's reputation was one of a miserable, mean and moody individual who was not welcomed here in life. However, the man who is said to haunt this place is considered quite friendly, he may be a practical joker at times but seems quite happy here. To Judy there is but one possible answer to the identity of the ghost, that of Walter (Wally) Trow himself, a short stocky man who was landlord of the Mug House for forty-four years.

A psychic who visited the pub reported a sadness upstairs, a feeling of the loss of an infant. Judy had never heard of such a case; as far as she was aware Wally had been a father of two children who had both lived long and quite contented lives. However, she was shocked to learn from one elderly villager who used the Mug as his local, that there had been a third child who had died a month before reaching its first birthday, but he could not recall if it was a son or daughter.

The psychic also reported another, previously unknown, presence with links to the days when the place was a brew house for the neighbouring church. It has long been thought that a tunnel existed between the two most important buildings in Claines, even if the construction itself had never been found.

Beneath the ground was also said to linger the spirit of a man. Sweating, frightened, nervous, he was wearing a long coat with many buttons and was on the run from the Battle of Worcester and had hidden in the tunnel. Perhaps he had been a local man, thus was aware of the existence of the tunnel which made a good hiding place. Yet it had one drawback, one could not see or hear any pursuers and thus any potential trap. His presence was sensed by the psychic, as was his end, for the man was said to have burned to death in his hiding place which was subsequently sealed.

As far as anyone knows, the tunnel and its remains are still beneath the ground here today.

COLWALL

Haunted Lane

Less than six months after the outbreak of the Second World War, a young lady was cycling home through Colwall. It had been a pleasant evening, one which had done something to lift her spirits. For the second time in a quarter of a century the nation was again at war, yet for a few hours this young lady had managed to put the thoughts of war to the back of her mind.

Arriving at a narrow road in the village, dubbed Haunted Lane by the locals, she met a frightening sight which must have been quite terrifying. Along her route came a procession of monks wearing habits with the hoods up. They carried between them the body of a young man which was draped in a black cloth. Glad of her speed advantage she turned those pedals as fast as she could to get her away from something which simply could not be.

As the bike sped down the lane she was overtaken by a galloping horse ridden hard by a man who was obviously as traumatised by the monks as she was. Ignoring the woman on the bicycle completely, he fled passed her, keen to put as much distance between himself and the procession as he possibly could.

If it was unusual for her to see a horse moving at such a speed late at night, it was nothing compared to her disbelief at seeing both horse and rider vanish into thin air on reaching the old railway bridge.

Were the two sights related in some way, or were they totally independent? With the absence of any other reports it is impossible to say.

COW HONEYBOURNE

Fleeting Visitor

During the days of steam a railway worker had returned to his cottage one evening after work. He was enjoying a quiet conversation with a friend when his dog began scratching at the kitchen door asking to be let through. Of course the man obliged and followed his faithful dog into the kitchen. Seated at the table was a man – hazy, misty, but certainly a man and one he did not recognise. The dog did not react adversely to the stranger; indeed the animal did not react at all, not even when they disappeared moments later.

No explanation for the event has ever been offered, nor has any possible identity of the man ever been suggested. Unless he returns the puzzle will never be solved.

CROPTHORNE

Holland House

Holland House, a delightful thatched building dating from the Tudor period, has been home to many over the centuries. The name is not an old one; it refers to the family who last owned it. One of the last of the Hollands to live here was not born into the family but married into it. Widowed comparatively young, she continued to live in the house she had grown to love for many years after the death of her husband.

Just a few short years after her death the house was sold on and, as a result, many more people visited the house. Was it the increased numbers which disturbed her sufficiently for her to return to her home after her death? Whatever the reason, it was reported on more than one occasion that the familiar figure of Mrs Holland was spotted from the gardens. Looking through the window from the library, her eyes wander across the courtyard and its lovely patchwork beds of roses and perennials which can have changed little since her occupancy.

Holland House

DROITWICH

Badly Parked

There has been a lot of redevelopment in Droitwich around the shopping centre and Victoria Square, bringing the area up to date. The modern library and heritage centre contrast tastefully with the black and white buildings of the Raven Hotel and its adjacent offices.

It has often been the case that unexplained activity is experienced more regularly following redevelopment of an area or refurbishment of a particular building. Perhaps this was the reason for this story which comes from 2007. It was late afternoon, and a man had just left work and driven around to collect his partner from her place of employment. She asked him to stop off in Victoria Square to use the cash machine and, with all the short-term parking bays occupied, he nipped into the empty bays for disabled parking on the opposite side of the road from the Raven Hotel. He admitted it gave him a very uneasy feeling but, as there was clearly no queue for the cash dispenser, his partner would be literally seconds and he would leave the engine ticking over.

It was late September and, while it was still light, the evening gloom was closing in on a rather dismal grey, but so far dry, day. Glancing around to ensure he had not been observed he did not notice anyone approaching. However, a movement out of the corner of his eye caught his attention; he turned quickly and saw a man approaching the passenger door from an angle slightly behind the car. His sudden shock turned to an uneasy feeling when he realised the man was strangely dressed in 'out of time clothing'.

Wearing what he thought were typically nineteenth-century working clothes, the man advanced slowly yet purposefully. The brown coarse cloth of his trousers, into which he had thrust his hands, was topped by a collarless white(ish) shirt and high-buttoned waistcoat. His face stuck out from underneath his 'bowler-style hat', a large hooked nose was dwarfed by a great moustache which spread across his face until it blended with the mutton-chop whiskers. As he came closer the man realised how much he towered over the car, he appeared to be around 7ft in height.

His height was accentuated further by his close proximity and, on reflection, his gait seemed strange. It appeared he was bouncing in slow motion, almost walking on air, which may account for his apparent great height. However, it was when the figure reached the car that the driver got his biggest shock, for without faltering a single step he walked straight through the bonnet of the car, even with the engine running.

The figure continued through the car and in an unerring straight line off towards the far side of the bank until the by now rigid driver lost sight of him. Had it not been for the seat belt he would have shot out of his seat when the passenger door opened that moment, his partner had returned with her cash. Visibly shaken he told her everything, yet, despite being only a few short yards from the car, she had seen nothing.

The black and white Raven Hotel. The parking bays marked out in the foreground is where the tall stranger appeared.

However, she was allowed to take the wheel for the short journey home, one of the very few times she had ever driven his car when he was a passenger. Furthermore he swore this was the last time he ever parked illegally.

Norbury Theatre

For many years Norbury Theatre was the Norbury Hotel and rumours persisted of unexplained events that happened there. It was maintained that there were bricked-up tunnels leading from the cellars of the old property to the local church. These stories were recalled when someone found a stone tablet in the churchyard of St Augustine's apparently reading 'TO THE NORBURY'. At last the tunnels were found and plans were made to dig down and open the route once more.

Some concerns were raised as to the wisdom of opening the tunnels again; it was rumoured that several bodies had been bricked up inside and they would have represented a very real risk of disease. However, when expert help was sought it was pointed out that any idea of a tunnel leading from the churchyard to underneath the hotel was at the very least imaginative. There is a drop of some 25m or more from the churchyard to the walkway below, making any 'tunnel' a shaft dropping vertically. Furthermore, it would then have to cut below the railway, the Droitwich Canal, the

This view of St Augustine's does not show how precipitous the drop is, thus a tunnel is not possible.

Salwarpe River and the road before coming anywhere near the theatre. The idea of any tunnel completely evaporated when, having cleaned the stone tablet, it revealed this was no tunnel entry but a marker for the tomb of the Norbury family.

However, this has not stopped reports of ghostly shadows and shapes being seen around the theatre. Neither has it silenced the mysterious bumps and bangs, nor controlled the temperature fluctuations.

Cavalier

During 1979 a number of residents in and around the newer development on the Chawsen housing estate reported seeing an old resident of the area. At the time they asked that their identities be kept secret and that request shall continue to be respected.

It the space of a few short weeks a number of tenants reported seeing a man dressed in clothes associated with a Cavalier inside their new homes. One individual was watching television as he was eating his evening meal. He stared in amazement as the figure paused in his living room almost directly between him and the evening news, looked about him, and then continued on to walk straight through the wall. By the time the occupant had recovered sufficiently to continue eating, his chips were quite cold.

Apart from the location and the visitor's attire, observers all agree that the man seemed unaware of the people and places about him and also that he appeared puzzled, even lost.

Priory House

At the end of Friar Street we find Priory House, an Elizabethan building with a chimney dating from the early eighteenth century. The place has been wonderfully restored, even the original colouring has been brought back to life – the building is more beige and brown than starkly black and white.

The house has long been said to be haunted, although the tales are conflicting. Some maintain the place has been quieter since the restoration, others quite the reverse. Often building work, decoration, or simply rearranging the furniture are said to be the catalyst for increased activity. And while the restoration of the place may have stirred up the resident ghost, it is also possible that returning the place to its former state has had a calming influence on the resident spirit.

Local legend tells several stories of the reasons for the ghost of Priory House: one maintains he was a former occupant who was unfairly ejected by the owner; a second says he committed suicide; a third that he died of an illness and a fourth maintains that he was killed. Another tale speaks of it being the ghost of a felon who was hanged for his crimes – again the stories diverge here: it is claimed he was a murderer, a highwayman, a thief, a traitor, and several other crimes which all carried a death sentence. However, there are also versions which speak of him in almost every one of these situations as being of the opposite gender.

Yet there was one local who suggested, maybe none too seriously, an explanation for the identity of the former occupant. It seems he believed the ghost was that of a former occupant, a hen-pecked husband whose life was made an utter misery by the vilest virago of a wife. It is this explanation which seems best suited to the mischievous disposition of the Priory House ghost, and also interests the author most of all, however it cannot be discounted that this may simply be because the story was tailored to fit the evidence.

The ghost seems intent on causing as much inconvenience as it possibly can. Small items, especially those which have a specific place, such as in a cabinet or on a shelf, are moved so as to be obviously out of place. This is also true of protective or decorative cloths on tables or chairs which, even if only slightly misaligned, stand out like the proverbial sore thumb. Rugs, too, have been found askew, although there has not been anyone around to move them. Doors and windows left open have been known to slam shut while, less easy to explain, those closed have suddenly burst open. Taps have irritatingly been found dripping when it is known they were turned off beforehand, while other items left in the bathroom are later found left untidily.

As we can see this haunting can hardly be said to be anything more than that of a prankster, something which this character clearly continues to enjoy.

EVESHAM

Abbey Bells

A church has stood here at Evesham since at least AD 700. The site was chosen by St Ecgwine, and is said to have been seen by him in a vision. Since the Dissolution of the Monasteries by Henry VIII only the Norman bell tower and the gateway remain.

The bell tower contains no bells; presumably they were either hidden by the monks or taken as spoils by the King's men. However, the pealing of bells is still heard by some every year on Christmas Eve.

Trumpet Inn

There is some dispute as to the origins of the Trumpet Inn, however there is no doubt that some parts of this building are very old. With the name of Trumpet it was thought to be an old coaching inn, yet there is another school of thought which points to this being a part of the old Abbey buildings. If the latter is the correct origin then this name comes from an association with the Archangel Gabriel.

When speaking to the landlady of the premises, Wendy Cope, she revealed the family's arrival in the summer of 2007 was overseen by her ever-present personal

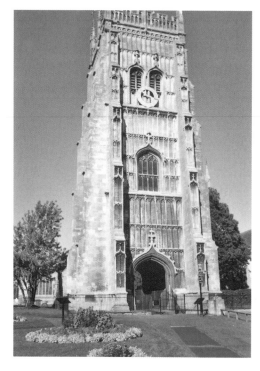

The tower is all that remains of Evesham's Abbey.

Resplendent hanging baskets outside the Trumpet Inn.

guardian. Over the last fourteen years, ever since the death of her father, whenever they have taken over the reigns of a new venture she has always sensed her father's presence. Soon after they had arrived at the Trumpet a psychic was visiting and revealed that 'Dad' had taken up residence in the pub. He was seated in a position so as to be able to watch the door and thus protect his loved ones.

The new spirit is not likely to suffer loneliness here as there is a second ghostly figure who seems to reside around the stairwell. For years her presence has been sensed, said to be a sadness of a kind – although they could not say why they thought it was female. Then last year one man, who has been a customer of the inn for over thirty years, glimpsed the maiden. She was described as a young woman of around twenty years of age, wearing clothing which was indistinct yet long, flowing and of a light colour. This sighting did not last for long and she has not, as far as anyone knows, been seen before or since.

Yet the most famous ghostly resident of all is a former landlord, who has revealed his presence on more than one occasion and in a number of different ways. During the 1960s Mr John Brown was a renowned practical joker, a popular man whose loss was felt by all who knew him. The manner of his death was particularly sad. As he entered the cellar he switched on the light in order to see what he was doing. What he did not notice until it was too late was the water flooding the cellar. With his hand on the switch he completed the circuit and the resulting electric shock killed him instantly.

It did not take long for Mr Brown to return to his beloved pub. Several times the electrics have been switched off in the cellar, cutting power to the pumps and interrupting the flow of beer to the bars above. However, it was when the daughter of the establishment was in the cellar one day when the oddest event occurred. While all the lights were on a heavy barrel of lager scraped and tottered its way across the cellar, almost as if it was being moved by someone, although nobody was anywhere near.

It seems that although Mr Brown is no longer running the pub he, and his renowned sense of humour, is going to be here for some time to come.

Priceless Shoes

Despite the threat of the dreaded Millennium Bug, the dawn of the year 2000 was a spectacle some may remember fondly and not the unmitigated disaster foretold by the doom merchants. However, in a quiet corner of Evesham the forecasts of doom seem to have awoken one previously unknown individual.

A few days before the end of the last millennium, a busy shoe shop in the High Street received its first of many visits. Current manageress Sandra Braithwaite explained how new shoes, still in the box, began to shoot off the shelves in the store room. The sound of the stock being tossed around the room could be heard downstairs in the shop, yet nobody was in the room at the time.

Recently, when an employee from another branch was covering for a holidaying staff member, came the only recorded example of flying boxes outside the stock room. Having to re-stock the shelves following the day's sales, he climbed upstairs to the stock room and began to remove the required shoes and stack them at the top of the stairs. When the list was complete he carried the first armful of boxes down to the shop. As soon as he had exited the stairwell the remaining shoe boxes shot from top to bottom and, judging by the noise, must have hit most of the wooden steps on the way down.

Since his first appearance, visits by Tom, as he has been christened, have been very frequent. Indeed he announces his presence on two or three days every week. However, he is not an early riser for the incidents never begin before 4.30 p.m., an hour before the shop closes.

The shop is not housed in a modern building, as evidenced by the cellar which provides further storage space as required. Although staff avoid entering the cellar if at all possible, every time they do they are aware of the unmistakable sweet aroma of lingering pipe tobacco smoke, as if the smoker had only moments ago vacated the room.

While permanent staff are wary of their visitor, they are not fearful of him; they sense nothing malevolent about Tom. Not so the temporary member of staff, for although he finished his stint as holiday cover, at the end of the week he vowed never to return.

Butcher at the Prison

During 2008 there were a number of unexplained occurrences at a shop in the High Street. Indeed, this is next door to the shoe shop of the previous narrative. Evesham's ghostly residents, as we have seen, are not shy in making their presence known and yet this particular building has been quiet for some time.

The building itself, now a perveyor the finest meats, was used as a prison during the seventeenth century. It was shortly after the Restoration of the Monarchy and the Quakers were under religious persecution. A number were arrested and held on these premises awaiting trial, although not all were happy with the treatment of the prisoners. It is on record that they were held in the dark and dismal dungeons, and fed the bare minimum to keep them alive. Such atrocious conditions are known to have resulted in the death of several before they ever saw a jury.

Several times doors have been known to slam shut, especially when the place is empty and thus very quiet. Footsteps were recently heard crossing the floorboards of an upstairs room, although it was known there was nobody else around. Could these be the result of the lingering spirits of those who died in the dungeon?

George

Towards the end of the twentieth century a Victorian house in Evesham was converted into two separate properties to cater for the demand for properties for the younger generation. Sharing a 'pad' with a good friend gave a certain amount of freedom and introduced the individual to the weight of financial responsibility.

The two girls who lived in this particular property, however, found that they were not alone. On the first day in the flat one of the girls walked up to the front door and saw an elderly man in uniform sitting outside the property, she greeted him, assuming that he was her friend's grandfather. To her indignation the 'misery' ignored her and, when she found her friend in their kitchen, she told her of the man seated outside their home. Her friend insisted her grandfather had been nowhere near the place and, after hearing the description, said it was the resident ghost. George, as he was christened, was often felt joining whoever was seated on the couch, the cushion sinking under the weight of an invisible guest. Neither of the young ladies was bothered by the haunting, for the most part the incidents were harmless and did not interfere with their daily lives.

The upstairs property was said to be haunted by a number of young girls and a woman, perhaps a governess or a teacher. The girls were often said to be dancing around, one resident claimed to be able to see them while another could only hear them.

The two flatmates shared the only bedroom and its one double bed. When one of the girls returned home late one night she crept into their bedroom and, seeing the sleeping form of her friend snuggled beneath the bedclothes, made as little noise as possible. At about 2 a.m. the next morning she was awoken by a loud and insistent knock at the front door. Sensibly asking who it was before opening the door at night she was surprised to learn it was the friend she had thought asleep in their bed. Indeed when she returned there was no sign that anyone had even in the bed that night.

Other strange events include levitating socks dancing around the room in the depth of night, while one resident claimed to have been bodily lifted from the floor by unseen arms.

FECKENHAM

Merry-Come-Sorrow Hill

Anyone who has read other books by the author will be aware of his interest in place names, particularly those names which give a glimpse of the history of the place. Can you imagine then his delight at finding a ghost story which gave rise to a place name?

Over the years a story has been passed down by word of mouth of a ghostly procession witnessed by several people over the centuries. A wedding party is seen ascending the slope yet, later that day, the return journey is that of a funeral. Events began many years ago when as happy a bride as could ever be imagined joined her friends and family for her big day. However, one witness did not share her joy. A witch, jealous of the young woman, cursed her and as she left the church a married woman she promptly fell down dead. Look closely as the ghostly procession descends and you will notice the bride still in her wedding gown, carried down the slope and borne to the door of her mother's home.

Questions have been asked as to where the party are heading for the ceremony and why they are crossing the field and not walking along the road. The first is difficult to answer, yet the fields would often have offered an easier route for the roads which were often made impassable due to the horse-drawn vehicles churning up the surface after a period of rain.

GREAT MALVERN

The Shadow of Ragged Stone Hill

In the fourteenth century a monk named John committed a sin. He broke his vows made when joining the order by seeking the company of a woman. His punishment was to climb and descend Ragged Stone Hill on his hands and knees, saying his prayers as he did so. This he was to do every day, no matter what the weather or his physical condition.

After many long months John's sanity failed. He ascended the hill for the last time, putting a curse on the hill, on those who had punished him and all those associated with them. With that he fell down dead, his body dissipating to form a dark column of dust or smoke. As it rose into the sky it swelled to form a vast dark cloud which cast a shadow across the land in the form of the monk. Thereafter anyone allowing the shadow of the hill and/or its standing stones to fall upon their person would risk any number of atrocities to fall upon them.

One family seemed particularly susceptible to the wrath of the fallen monk. The residents of Birtsmorton Court, who had enjoyed a close and mutually beneficial relationship with the friary for many years, lost their eldest son and heir suddenly and

The view from Ragged Stone Hill.

The ragged stones are not likely to throw much of a shadow.

seemingly without any cause. Some reports tell how the family were eventually forced to leave their home in order to escape their tormentor.

Today the shadow still looms over the region and visitors will do well to avoid the chilling darkness cast by the hill and the accursed stone.

Shade of Druidism

A remarkably similar warning to that of previous story of Friar John is told about the Druids who are said to have made their last stand against the invading Romans. As the enemy tightened their grip around them and defeat was inevitable they are said to have raised their faces to the sky and cast their curse on all who would dare to approach their sacred place. Ever since a menacing shade has been said to drift around the hill tops, appearing to be lost and confused.

This narrative seems to have elements from that of Friar John and the last stand of Caractacus, as told under Little Malvern. Furthermore the Druids, said to have 'raised their faces to the sky', considered the next world to be reached by going down not up and would have sought help from the gods of the earth, not the heavens.

GRIMLEY

Elizabeth

After the annual office Christmas get-together Mark drove home. While he had eaten heartily, he had not touched a drop of alcohol. Four of his colleagues lived some distance away, in the same general direction, and he had volunteered to do the driving.

The route he took meant taking country lanes which, while he had travelled them many times before, he was obviously not as familiar with as he was with his normal route. Thus he was driving at no more than 45mph, the road was wet but it was not raining and visibility was good. When Mark noticed a pedestrian in his headlights he courteously dipped them and slowed still more so he could pass safely. His speed was little more than 30mph when his headlights picked up a dishevelled and clearly distressed young woman at the side of the road. Mark stopped a little further along and, wary of not worrying her by approaching her, stood next to his vehicle and called out to ask if she needed help. The girl was sobbing loudly and, if she did respond, her words were unintelligible.

Taking a few steps forward he attempted to reassure her and asked if he could call for an ambulance or the police, but the very mention of the police seemed to bring about a panic attack. Remaining at a discrete distance he continued to talk to her, and eventually she calmed sufficiently for Mark to understand her name was Elizabeth and she lived just over a mile away. She insisted she did not require the emergency services but would welcome a lift home. In the low light of the car Mark could make out a number of scratches on her hands and face which appeared superficial, yet her pallor was disturbing. She appeared to be about twenty years of age and during the short journey Mark kept her talking so the time passed more quickly for her. He learned she had been out with her boyfriend on his motorcycle. They had had an argument and, for reasons unclear, she had been abandoned at the side of the road. Just then they reached her home. She thanked him and he waited in the car until she had limped up the path and closed the door behind her.

Something about Elizabeth's colour perturbed him and he found sleep hard to come by that night. Next day was Saturday and, still with Elizabeth on his mind, he and his wife took a detour to Grimley on their way to the shops to enquire as to Elizabeth's health. Together they knocked on the door and were greeted by a man in his seventies and, as he listened to their brief narrative of the previous night, his jaw fell. The older gentleman, visibly shocked, then told them of how there used to be a girl who lived there called Elizabeth. However, she had been murdered by her boyfriend and left in the hedgerow at the side of the road, the very road Mark had driven along the previous Friday night. That was thirty years ago.

Incidentally, the place name of Grimley is derived from Old English *grima hyll* and means '(the place at) the hill of the ghost or spectre'.

HAGLEY

Lord Lyttleton

Hagley Hall is one of the loveliest stately homes in the land. Set in a varied and rolling landscape, new wonders are revealed at every turn. A delightful mix of flowerbeds, winding paths, woodland and water have provided artists with inspirational views.

Within the house itself more delights are found in every room. Its architecture and decoration are among the finest in the land and the thousands of visitors it receives each and every year are adequate testimony to the work done by the inhabitants since the Lytteltons family built the first house and laid out the original gardens.

The Lyttelton's have been around Worcestershire since the twelfth century and possibly longer. However, our story starts on 30 January 1744 and the birth of Thomas, who was destined to become the second Lord Lyttelton. He was only in his third year when his mother died and his subsequent childhood was overseen by a succession of tutors and distant family members.

Reaching his adulthood he was a source of great displeasure to his father. He lived a wild life, given over to questionable conduct which, while not illegal, was not that befitting a man of his birth. However, this was common among the young men of his age and he was by no means the worst of his generation. On the death of his father in 1773 the title passed to him, although his erratic behaviour in his early life led to him being more commonly referred to as 'The Bad Lyttelton' or even 'The Wicked Lyttelton'.

On his return from office in Ireland he was already suffering ill health, fits, headaches, and chronic indigestion which was more likely heart disease. His life was made bearable through medicines and regular bed rest, particularly following a fit. It was on one such occasion in 1779 that he retired early to bed on the night of 24 November. A servant brought him the medicine and left him when ordered to do so.

Thomas had not been alone for long when he was disturbed by the fluttering of wings within the room. He listened and heard footsteps approaching his bed whereupon he sat up and was stunned to see the loveliest woman he had ever seen standing alongside his bed. Clad all in white she had a small bird perched on her hand and she spoke to him. He was speechless as he heard her tell him to prepare himself for death. When he enquired how long he had she replied by midnight on the third day.

Next morning his discomfort was evident and, over breakfast, he told his guests of the events of the previous night. He dismissed it as a dream, saying how he had forgotten to release a robin trapped in the greenhouse a few days before, which was clearly still playing on his mind. Any chance of convincing everyone else the matter was but a trivial one was made impossible by his evident stress and low spirits.

However, later that day his mood was much improved and he made two quite superb speeches in the House of Lords. The second and third days also saw him in fine form, both in mind and body. Yet by the time they were seated for dinner the gloom was again descending.

His friends and colleagues, concerned that the woman in white's prophecy may lead to tragedy, contrived to get every clock and watch in the place put forward by thirty minutes. Thus when Lord Lyttelton retired at what he thought was half past eleven, feeling drawn and exhausted, it was only eleven o'clock. As the appointed hour approached Lyttelton repeatedly checked clocks to ensure they were still working.

Eventually, when his watch read fifteen minutes after midnight and, confident that he was now safe, he summoned his valet to bring him his medicine. Soon however, from the next room the servant heard the unmistakeable sounds of laboured breathing, he returned to find the life ebbing from his master. Summoning help, Lyttelton's cousins, including Lord Fortescue, ran to the bedside. They arrived just in time to see the death of Thomas Lyttelton at the moment the clocks all said half past twelve, in reality midnight – exactly as foretold by the ghost in white.

Meanwhile, at the very moment of his death, Lyttelton appeared at the side of the bed of a Mr Andrews, one of his closest friends. Andrews thought it some sort of prank and rang for a servant to prepare a room immediately. By the time the servant arrived Andrews was alone. He dressed and organised a thorough search. However the news of Thomas Lyttelton's demise came in the form of a messenger, telling of the passing of the peer at the age of thirty-five.

It has been suggested that the woman in white was Lyttelton's mother. Yet although he could not have had any recollection of her (as she died when he was very young), he would certainly have seen her portrait hanging in his home, so he would surely have recognised her.

Since that time there have not been any similar reports of hauntings at Hagley, so her identity remains a mystery.

HANBURY

Emma Vernon

Hanbury Hall was home to the Vernon family from the fifteenth century, the present house being built at the beginning of the eighteenth century.

The subject of our story was the only child of Thomas Vernon and Emma Cornwall. Thomas died in 1771 when his daughter was just sixteen years old. Five years later her mother had found her a husband, Henry Cecil, eldest son of the Earl of Exeter. However, the marriage was virtually doomed from the start and Emma sought solace in curate William Sneyd. Before her fourth wedding anniversary Emma had eloped to Portugal with the curate, and Henry was left to sort out the financial mess left behind. In its day this was a huge scandal, providing a great deal of subject matter for gossips for some considerable time.

It was a further twelve years before Emma and Henry divorced, leaving her free to marry her beloved William in 1791. The marriage lasted just two years, consumption taking the life of Emma's second husband and forcing her to return home penniless. Back in Hanbury Emma approached John Phillips, a local solicitor, to attempt to make some sense of her affairs. She made him her third husband two years later.

In 1818 Emma Vernon lay dying and sent for a trusted former maid. She requested she be buried wrapped in the same blanket she had used when nursing her second husband William. At the age of sixty-three her request was granted and she was buried just outside Hanbury Churchyard in unconsecrated ground. This may well have been a mistake, for her ghost is still seen roaming around the lanes of Hanbury and particularly the Hall and grounds.

Around Hanbury Emma has most often been seen walking along Church Avenue. This would have been the path taken by her in order to see the then curate, William Sneyd. A woman driving along here once stopped to offer a woman a lift, thinking it surely could not be safe to walk such desolate roads alone day or night. However, when she pulled over alongside her the woman had vanished. Not long afterwards a campanologist was leaving the church following bell-ringing practice. As he left he glanced back and noticed a figure of pure white walk along the path and disappear through the very door he had just locked. Although it was night, visibility was quite good for there was a bright moon and his eyes were well-accustomed to the gloom.

Emma's appearances around the church and Hall never are never described as being in any way malevolent, indeed she keeps herself very much to herself. However, one local inn, the Country Girl, has also claimed Emma to be responsible for their unexplained phenomena and yet the actions of this ghost seem quite a different character – as we shall see on the following page.

Sir George

With Emma's death in 1818 ownership of Hanbury Hall passed to a distant branch of the family. Eventually Sir George Vernon took possession in 1920; he was to be the last Vernon in residence. An eccentric man, he left everything he had to the daughter of the farm foreman, whom he had trained as his secretary and introduced as a member of his own family.

He fought a constant battle with the Church throughout his life. He was particularly outspoken against tithes, especially after he discovered his personal belongings outside his home as part of an auction to raise money to pay his dues. His dislike of the Church explains why he requested he was buried in unconsecrated ground in Shrawley Wood. Furthermore he asked to be buried with his rifle, which may be a clue he had already decided to take his own life.

Sir George shot himself with his own rifle in the Blue Bedroom of Hanbury Hall in 1940. He was suffering from ill-health and his advancing years put constraints on him he found unbearable. The eccentric gentleman still makes regular appearances around the Hall; a member of staff noted his presence in the very room he took his own life as recently as 2003.

Country Girl Inn

During the 1980s the landlord of the Country Girl claimed that this was the most haunted public house in the country; whilst it may have seemed so to him at the time, the author has certainly encountered places where paranormal reports are more frequent.

The most common occurrence were footsteps heard climbing the bare wooden stairs and walking toward the bedroom. Nothing else was heard; the door never opened, nobody knocked, nor were the footsteps heard walking away. Another event happened in the kitchens, just as the girl who worked there was starting her shift. A creak behind her attracted her attention. As she turned she saw four plates fly from where they were stored on the wall and land several feet away, somehow without incurring any damage whatsoever.

When collecting his girlfriend from the inn at the end of her shift one night, a young man parked outside in the car park at the rear of the pub. Nearby a small ornamental pool was in sight. Suddenly he was aware of a white misty shape rising from the water. Terrified, the poor man ran into the pub seeking safety in numbers. It seems it was upwards of twenty minutes before he came close to regaining his composure.

Eight Days at the Country Girl

Tim Churchman arrived at Hanbury eager to face the challenge that awaited him as the new landlord of the Country Girl. As regulars are so fond of doing, they soon impressed upon the new boss their knowledge of the place as it is and also its history.

Included in this was the story of how a former occupant had warned that should the sign which gave the pub its name ever be removed from the premises she would return to haunt the place.

This story was greeted with a knowing smile and a courteous 'Thank you' and mostly ignored. The sign, which remains a perfect representation of the name, had been adorned with the name of the Whitbread brewery at some time during the 1950s and was out of place under the new ownership. Hence the sign was removed and held in storage until a local farmer approached Tim and asked if he could have the sign. He explained that his family had farmed this area for over 250 years and his ancestors would have enjoyed a pint of ale or three here when the place first opened in 1860, as he himself had done ever since he enjoyed his first pint at the very establishment. Feeling the farming generations would appreciate the image much more, Tim generously handed the sign over and the farmer took home the cherished sign. He was to retain the gift for all of eight days.

Very soon after things began to happen and always seemingly when the new landlord was alone in the building. After hours a glass in the front door of the pub smashed without reason, the glass was quite thick and would have required a substantial blow to break it and yet no evidence of any missile or weapon could be traced. A couple of days later a sink overflowed, the dirty water coming back up through the waste pipe although that sink had not been used for as long as anyone could recall.

It was 2 a.m. one morning when Tim had his next message and, as it transpired, the one which finally brought about the decision to retrieve the sign. He was working in the cellar, preparing for the cleaning of the pipes the next day, when the circuit breakers tripped and every light in the place went out. Not having a light to work by

The sign which caused all the trouble at the Country Girl, Hanbury.

was a little disconcerting and the catalyst which saw him request the return of the sign the next day.

Today the sign is back at the Country Girl, still not hung because of the outdated brewery name emblazoned across it, but safe back in the pub which has been quiet, at least in a spiritual sense, ever since.

HANLEY CASTLE

One Old House

One resident of Hanley Castle, whom we shall call Trevor, has investigated the history of his house and its former occupants. The place is centuries old and has seen much change in the village.

Trevor's interest in the history of the place began on the first night he stayed in the property. After a long and extremely tiring day the family were winding down. Still charged by the adrenalin of that long day, sleep was not coming easily and a book and a drink accompanied them to their beds. The main bedroom was constructed in the eaves of an old hall, above what had become the drawing room. About thirty minutes after midnight the couple heard sounds coming from the room below them. It was the unmistakable sound of a chair being dragged across the wooden floor.

Not having been around the property for long enough to install any security devices, Trevor's first thought was they had burglars. With just his wife and young family in the house, their safety uppermost in his mind; he thought quickly and as he ran down the stairs he made a great deal of noise and clearly shouting, 'C'mon Dave, we have to get the burglars!' to suggest there was more than one adult male present. However, when he reached the drawing room and flung open the door no burglars were to be seen. Inside the large room all that could be seen were boxes, no furniture had been placed there as they had yet to decide what to do with the room, and there was certainly no chair.

Since that first night they have settled in and the drawing room is undoubtedly now the nicest room in the house, although it is only normally used when the family have guests. However, it is always noticeably colder in this room than anywhere else in the property and a log fire is always burning in the colder months to raise the temperature those few degrees. Above this room is still the main bedroom and it was here that footsteps were heard walking across the floor of the loft or attic. Yet there is not enough space in the roof of the building for it to be possible to walk along the roof in this way.

Asking questions in and around the village – particularly at the wonderful local of the Three Kings which retains a unique rustic charm and (as the author can confirm) the warmest of welcomes together with an array of the realest of ales – Trevor discovered something of the more recent occupants. The family who had been here before had, not unexpectedly, failed to mention they had bought the place from a couple who had been perturbed by the recurring sounds of girls playing and running around. The sounds had disturbed them so often they had resorted to having the place exorcised. It was then

One of the picturesque properties at Hanley Castle.

they discovered that the large hall – now split into Trevor's drawing room and master bedroom – had once been used as the venue for the weekly Sunday school.

Since the initial disturbance on that first night Trevor and his family have seen, nor heard, little or no activity. Indeed the only recurring sign seems to be the cold felt in the drawing room. Interestingly, even though the master bedroom occupies the same space as the hall it does not exhibit the same feeling of cold felt in the drawing room below.

HANLEY CHILD

Norgrove

The Cookes family came to England with the Normans, probably arriving before the end of the eleventh century, and they have been consistently among the richest of Worcestershire's families ever since. It is popularly believed that the red hand in the family's coat of arms signifies a murderer – and is often said to be 'a sign of Cain'.

One head of the household (although some versions give it as the heir to the estates) is said to have murdered his groom in a fit of rage and buried his victim under a large tree at Norgrove. Within one room, always said to be colder than the rest of the building, any candle or flame lit or carried here would instantly be extinguished. A sudden gust of air, even in a room without an open door or window, would blow the flame out.

HARVINGTON CROSS

Mistress Hicks

Although the stories surrounding the infamous Mistress Hicks are told as being centred on Harvington Hall, she spreads her wings further – as we shall see.

Known by all the locals to be a witch, when anything untoward happened she was the obvious source of the problem. Sudden storms on the sunniest of days could have only been started by the witch. The blame for the spontaneous vomiting of pins by both the local women and children was firmly lodged with Mistress Hicks.

Eventually her spells and potions proved too much. Following a short, and likely unfair, trial she was found guilty of being a witch. Her punishment was carried out at the nearby main crossroads, where she was hanged.

If it was hoped her hanging would rid Harvington of their resident witch, the locals were a little premature. Within a few short weeks she was back. Ever since her ghost has been seen haunting the grounds of Harvington Hall and the surrounding lanes. If you see her give her a wide berth, for her mood does not seem to have improved.

Does Harvington village green hide a secret?

Harvington crossroads.

HINDLIP

Lady Hobbingdon

Nothing excites the ghost hunter more than a known date for an appearance and Hindlip Hall has just such a regular haunting.

The owner of this house as the seventeenth century gave way to the eighteenth was Thomas Hobbingdon. A fair and kind man, he had one dark secret – he was a Catholic, and as a result of his faith was condemned to death. However, he escaped the executioner when his wife wrote and informed the authorities of the Gun Powder Plot.

Hobbingdon returned to Hindlip, seemingly a reformed man. Yet behind the scenes things had changed little. Many old houses had secret rooms, which became known as priest holes for they were often used to hide Catholic priests from the authorities. This enabled them to carry on their religion and that of their benefactors. While such rooms were necessarily cramped, efforts were made to decorate them in a style appropriate as a place of worship.

Back at Hindlip two priests, Oldcorn and Gornet, were already hidden in the depths of the hall. Over the years many stories have been told of their exploits and adventures, most of which have clearly been greatly exaggerated. A succession of miraculous and quite extraordinary events meant they continued to evade capture.

However, Lady Hobbingdon, having saved her husband from the gallows, was blissfully unaware of what was going on under her very roof. The sounds she heard at night were a source of concern for her; she thought the place possessed and imagined all manner of evil within. A pure white calf, a garland of pearly white roses around its neck, was reported to be seen on numerous occasions.

One night it came and roused her from sleep, beckoning that she should follow. Through a series of passages, panels, stairs, secret rooms and trapdoors she was led, until she was completely lost. The calf stopped and promptly vanished, leaving just a piece of paper to fall to the floor. The lady of the house retrieved the scrap and found a single word written there, 'S.E.A.R.C.H.'.

Scared and lost, the woman stamped her foot in sheer exasperation. At once the oak of the chimney-piece slid to one side, just allowing passage to a hidden room. Peering in she saw Oldcorn and Gornet, almost starved to death. The shock of what she saw brought her to her senses and she made her way to the kitchen, returning with food and drink just as the great clock struck one.

Thereafter every night at exactly the same time she brought food to the men, the chiming of the clock masking the sound of her stamping her foot to open the panel. She soon became aware of other rooms and other occupants, whom she also brought a nightly share of food and water. For many years after her death she and the calf were seen gliding noiselessly in and out of the secret places in the Hall on the night of All Saints' Eve, better known today as Halloween.

A disastrous fire in 1818 resulted in the old building being demolished for safety reasons, any evidence of secret rooms and the occupants disappearing with it. Lady Hobbingdon was never seen again on 31 October or any other day of the year. Soon after the fire another figure was reported in the grounds. A young girl in a tartan dress is crying and said to be searching for her mother. Nobody has any idea who she may be or what connection she has with the estate of Hindlip Hall.

HINTON-ON-THE-GREEN

Manor House

The history of Manor House is a little sketchy. It appears to date from around the sixteenth century; however it is equally possible that a much older building is obscured behind the structural improvements and additions of later generations. What is clear, however, is that the building has been subject to some unusual goings-on.

It is reported that during the reign of Queen Victoria (1837–1901) footsteps were heard tramping around the building. Several individuals in the house were said to have heard these heavy footsteps and the route the footsteps took was always the same; they arrived at the front door and walked up the stairs. Indeed they were heard passing people standing on the staircase, yet nothing was ever seen nor did anyone report anything or anyone brushing past them. Slowly, deliberately, the sounds ascended all the way to the attic, when the unmistakable sound of the boots being kicked off and crashing on to the wooden flooring. So regular and so eerie were these sounds that servants refused to stay in the house, resulting in the place becoming empty and completely run down.

At the beginning of the twentieth century the older parts of the building were demolished. It seems this was the somewhat unusual solution to the haunted staircase, for since then there has not been a single reported occasion of the footsteps. However, this may simply be because nobody has been around to hear it.

HOLT

Holt Castle

All that remains of the original Norman castle of Holt are the foundations. The tower dates from the fourteenth century and the hall the fifteenth. Its location on the west bank of the River Severn would have been as much a prime location then as it is today.

Servants at the hall in Victorian times knew of the Lady in Black. This mysterious figure only ever appeared in one passageway near the attics. She was described as being quite tall and thin, walking very upright and striding slowly yet purposefully along

The imposing fourteenth-century tower of Holt Castle.

the corridor. Her dress was of a heavy black lace and drags on the ground behind her. Nobody knows who she may be or what she was doing here.

Perhaps she has some association with the raven in the cellars. This ill-tempered bird would attack anyone carrying a light source, clearly a necessity in the dark of the cellar. As the individual approached the cask the bird would flap its wings and extinguish the candle, thus leaving the visitor in the dark. At nearby Leigh Court to the south-west an identical story was admitted as having been created to dissuade those from venturing into the cellars to help themselves to the drink.

HUDDINGTON

Lady Winter

The number of similarities between this story and the narrative from Hindlip is not surprising. Tales of derring-do against all the odds by those involved in the Gunpowder Plot are found throughout the land, particularly around the Midlands.

Thomas Winter and his wife were a very happy couple. Unfortunately, their time together was not as long as they would have wished for the husband was soon to be a hunted man, wanted for his role in the Gunpowder Plot. The couple were forced to resort to surreptitious liaisons under the cover of darkness. The couple would take walks along the avenue of oak trees, a path they had taken many times before. This was to be Winter's undoing and he was arrested during one of the visits, thought to have been turned in by a servant at the house.

Although his was a relatively minor role, it was an act of treason and he soon faced the executioner. Grief has made Lady Winter a restless soul and, four centuries after her husband's death, she is still seen walking around the moat and between the old trees on the anniversary of the day Thomas died. She has also been spotted along Crowle Brook, a little away from the house.

However, all the sightings report her as being, like her husband – headless.

KEMPSEY

Battle of Worcester

On 3 September 1651 the two sides in the English Civil War faced each other on the battlefield north of Kempsey, between Powick and Worcester. It was to be one of the pivotal battles of the war; the day belonged to the 28,000 Parliamentarians who defeated the 16,000 Royalist troops. Of those who began the day fighting for their King, 10,000 were taken prisoner and 3,000 were killed during the battle that day.

Following the defeat the future King Charles II fled, evading capture by hiding in an oak tree near Boscobel House with his aide, Col. Carless. It is this hiding place which is commemorated by the pub name of Royal Oak, the second most popular name in the country.

Twenty-four hours earlier the troops were gathering for the engagement. South of Worcester is the village of Kempsey, which in the seventeenth century would have been even smaller than it is today. One of the Royalist troops, Fitzwilliam, had visited the area before and was aware of the existence of Kempsey. Indeed Fitzwilliam had other things on his mind that evening. As his companions busied themselves preparing their weapons, the soldier slipped away and rode south.

During a visit some years before, Fitzwilliam had befriended a certain young lady who had made his stay most welcome indeed. The soldier had not forgotten how accommodating she had been and was anxious to be re-united on the eve of battle. On his arrival he discovered that she was now living in a different house near to the church.

Powick Church observed the battle of 1651.

A few moments later the amorous soldier had left his horse to graze outside and was climbing the ivy-covered wall to the bedroom. Here he discovered her sleeping on the bed, her long fair hair framing her lovely face just as he had remembered. He awakened her and, to his delight, discovered she was as friendly as ever.

That next hour must have passed rather quickly, for they did not hear the back door of the cottage open, but they could not fail to hear a man's booming voice demanding to know what the horse was doing outside his home. Obviously the sight of the handsome young soldier had caused her more than a little confusion, for she had entirely forgotten to tell him about her marriage to the village blacksmith.

Tom Smithers, as befitting all blacksmiths, was big and very strong, in fact he was a giant of a man, said to have tipped the scales at over 130kg. Upstairs Fitzwilliam could not see the man, yet the sound of his voice was enough to tell him he would be fighting way beyond his weight. The sound of the husband's huge stomping feet upon the stairs spurred him into action. As Tom's silhouette appeared in the doorway the Cavalier pulled on his long boots, donned his hat and leapt through the open window.

For a split second the scene must have been rather amusing: a slightly built man, naked save for a resplendent hat and boots, plummeting from an upstairs window, accompanied by a terrifying angry roar from the throat of the owner of the house. Fitzwilliam's target when he leapt had been his horse; clearly his intention was to land neatly in the saddle and make a swift escape. Whether he had attempted this feat before is unknown, yet we do know he never had the chance to do so again. It has been suggested the roar from the upstairs window scared the horse, yet it is more likely that Fitzwilliam simply misjudged his leap. Whatever the reason, Fitzwilliam landed a few inches further forward than he intended and only succeeded in impaling himself between his legs on the pommel of the saddle.

It is said the man's scream was more terrifying than any heard on the battlefield the next day. The horrendous sound made the horse bolt and, as the man died, both sped off through the village in the direction of Kempsey Common.

Since then there have been several reports of ghostly sounds; a horse galloping at breakneck speed through the village, or the scream of the soldier simultaneously robbed of his life and his manhood. Others claim to have seen the steed careering across the Common, the dead man still clutching the reins, the horse swathed in its own sweat and the blood of its rider.

Three men stationed at Defford Airfield, which borders the other side of Kempsey Common, reported hearing a ghostly horse galloping across the land to the north-east.

Anyone thinking that death by saddle pommel is a little far fetched should know this is not the first time such a tragedy was recorded. Indeed, one of the most famous figures in British history suffered a similar fate. In September 1087 William the Conqueror was riding through the smouldering remains of a village in his native Normandy, when sparks made his horse rear up and the pommel rammed into the King's stomach. Unlike the ghostly soldier, William lived for several days before succumbing through massive internal injuries.

Ghost at the Gate

On a crisp and clear November evening two friends were out walking their dogs. The ladies were old friends, one still living in Kempsey the other returned just for the weekend to visit. The two had taken the opportunity of the walk to enable them to talk without their husbands.

Their route took them north along the main road through the village to the A38, where they turned left along the delightfully named Pixham Ferry Lane. Three hundred meters along this straight lane they turned left again on to Old Road South. At this junction one of the ladies felt the hairs on her neck rise and had the distinct impression they were being watched.

Across the way was a gate to a field. Leaning against this was the black silhouette of a male figure. As they looked they began to make out more detail. The figure was wearing hob-nailed boots, a neckerchief, and a waistcoat over an open-necked shirt. His cap was worn at the jauntiest of angles and on his face was a disarming and cheeky grin. Appearing to be aged around thirty-five years old, he was the perfect image of a Victorian farm labourer. The ladies were not in any way afraid, and were sure he was about to doff his cap and greet them politely, when he promptly vanished.

Later that evening, before they spoke to anyone, they both agreed to jot down a description of what they had seen. While the resident had made out much detail,

The junction of Old Road South …

… and Pixham Ferry Lane, where the gate once stood.

her guest had never seen more than the outline, described as a void through which nothing could be seen.

While it is not unusual to find individuals seeing different things, the reaction of their dogs is most unexpected. Many reports speak of how the family pet is aware of something which seems to be beyond our sensory range. In this insance, both ladies saw something and yet their canine companions paid not the slightest attention to the man, even though they would have expected them to bark a protective warning.

Manor House

The old manor house at Kempsey was a big building, too large for one family, and thus it was decided to redevelop it as two properties. Former occupants of the rear property spoke of how they had found a number of little things which, on reflection, could be considered mere coincidences. Yet when added to two other experiences, odd sensations, sounds and items being moved inexplicably, these little things seem relevant.

One room, described as 'the spookiest room' in the house, was where domestic tasks were performed. While the husband was ironing his shirts here one day, he heard his name being called and responded to the summons he thought had come from his wife. However, when he found her, she insisted she had not called his name and was not even aware he was still within the building. Moments later, having returned to the room and his ironing with his wife, he again heard his name being called. However, neither of them had spoken and they were the only people in the house.

Christmas is the traditional time for friends and family to gather together and celebrate. At the manor house one year a number had planned to spend the day together in the traditional manner – husbands down the local enjoying a pre-dinner drink, children playing, and wives preparing the meal and enjoying a glass of wine themselves. As the six women toiled in the spacious kitchen one door opened and, although nobody appeared, closed again behind an unseen visitor. The women watched in shocked silence as something crossed the room, disturbing a number of items of cutlery as they did so, before exiting through the other door which again opened and closed on its own accord.

When the husbands returned from the pub they found dinner somewhat delayed and six rather shaken partners.

KERSOE

Horsebridge Hill

It is November 1906; Edward VII is on the throne and the term 'world war' has not been heard. Two men are walking home from Badsey, it is a chilly evening just before ten o'clock and as they approach the bottom of the hill near a small stream they are met by what was later described as a 'female form'.

The encounter seems to have been unusual as this turned out to be one of those rare occasions when the ghost not only spoke but actually engaged in conversation.

The woman seemed to appear from nowhere and headed unerringly straight toward them. While one man walked on she stopped the other and, touching him on the shoulder, spoke, saying, 'You are Claude.'

'I'm not, I'm … from Evesham,' was his nervous response.

'You are Claude,' she insisted. 'You murdered me seventy-five years ago,' whereupon she promptly vanished. Justifiably frightened out of his wits, the man shouted out loud and ran to catch up with his companion.

Curiously, his colleague had not seen nor heard anything at all and was surprised when his friend ran and caught up with him trembling like a leaf.

Ghosts tend to stay close to the scene of a significant period or moment in their life. Thus I conducted some enquiries to see if I could discover if a woman was murdered near here, or if a woman from hereabouts had been killed, but I found nothing. A contemporary newspaper report about this encounter quite clearly states this 'ghost has appeared again' and yet, despite extensive searches, I could find no mention of another encounter. Thus I was forced to accept the woman's stated time frame and look for a possible victim from around 1830 and earlier. It came as no surprise to find there was no case which fit these clues.

Such a small place will have very few if any murder connections over hundreds of years, simply because there have been so very few people at Kersoe over the centuries. While it would be easy to dismiss it as being a misplaced ghost, perhaps we should also consider her a victim of a crime which was never discovered and hence she continued to seek her killer and bring Claude to justice.

KIDDERMINSTER

Harvey's Wine Bar

Swan Street had been the site of a wine bar for many years until its demolition for the new Swan Centre shopping centre. Whilst the wine bar was not particularly old, the building showed evidence of foundations from the Tudor period. During demolition a tunnel was discovered running from the cellars directly to St Mary's Church and two complete skeletons were uncovered during this work. Investigations revealed they had been here since the latter half of the sixteenth or early seventeenth centuries.

Neither of the skeletons appeared to be female, so these are not the Brown Lady who has been seen several times, wearing a brown dress and the white ruff typical of the Tudor period. On a number of occasions she has been seen walking straight through the horseshoe-shaped bar, the cash register and across the room. As with many ghosts she seems blissfully unaware of her modern surroundings or of anyone else in the room.

Other phenomena include the opening and closing of doors, even though there is nobody around. It remains to be seen if the Brown Lady was responsible for any of these events, yet since the place was demolished nothing has been seen or heard which could be described as paranormal activity.

However, this was not the first time the Brown Lady had surfaced in a licensed establishment here, for there is a very similar tale dating from 1851. At this time there was a public house known as the Clarence Inn on almost exactly the same site. Although it is difficult to gauge the old maps accurately it appears the two places, had they been contemporary, would have stood next door to each other. Furthermore the underground workings, both tunnels and cellars, were large enough to have served both premises at the same time.

In the mid-nineteenth century a strange woman was reported to have been seen crossing a room in the Clarence. At various times she was observed disappearing through a partition, a wall, and a closed door while carrying a tray containing food and drink. Again, being female, this cannot be the ghost of the skeletons but she is certainly not the same figure spotted in the wine bar a century later.

With the development of the Swan Centre it raises the question of what has happened to the long-term ghost of Swan Street. Does she still wander through the modern concrete and breeze block walls, or has the twenty-first-century development finally proved to be an impenetrable barrier?

A Murdered Landlady

Little is known of the individuals who appear in this narrative, the story having been passed down from generation to generation. Any tale which has not been committed to paper is likely to have errors and exaggerations creeping in.

In Kidderminster the Black Horse was a popular inn among those in the community. It was newly built and the landlady and her husband were enthusiastic and proud of their new establishment. They made every effort to make their customers feel most welcome.

However, the landlady overstepped the mark in the warmth of her welcome and was subsequently discovered on the steps of the pub, locked in a most passionate embrace with her lover. Her husband completely lost his temper and killed her where she stood.

Legend has it that for years afterwards her footsteps were heard pacing the corridors, her quick little steps recognisable as she flitted here and there ensuring her customers had everything they desired.

Ye Olde Seven Stars

Prior to the outbreak of the First World War, an unusual customer was spotted in the bar of Ye Olde Seven Stars in Coventry Street. The figure, a woman in her forties, wearing a white apron over a white dress of a design from the previous century, vanished within moments of being spotted. At no time did she interact with those in the bar, indeed she acted as if she was unaware of their presence.

Nothing more is recorded for another sixty years, until a spate of sightings occurred. This time reports made no mention of an apron, however the clothes are again said to be white and the woman of comparable age. Some reports have her standing at the bar, others seated, however all agree her appearances are brief and she vanishes in front of their eyes.

Kettle Conundrum

Among the rows of shops, where the banks, building societies and estate agents almost formed their own community, a mysterious visitor was seen in the 1980s.

At the Nationwide Building Society a succession of staff members witnessed a woman of around forty years of age in the back rooms of the building restricted to staff alone. The woman was described as wearing a long, light grey dress, with a cream-coloured apron over it, and a white mob cap. Her attire seems suitable for her actions, even in the modern era, for she seemed to be fascinated by the electric kettle and announced her presence by switching it on to boil. Nobody who has worked here has felt uncomfortable or threatened by the visitor. Indeed they have warmed to this woman, who has been known as Polly (for putting the kettle on), for her part in providing impromptu cups of tea and coffee.

LENCHWICK

Phantom Coach

On particular nights it is said that a phantom coach can be seen travelling along the driveway from the manor house at Lenchwick. Reaching the end of the drive it heads off at break-neck speed in the direction of Evesham Abbey. Fire is said to flare from the nostrils of the wild-eyed horses and the crack of the coachman's whip is heard, although neither man nor whip can be seen.

Within the carriage itself a ghostly figure can be seen at the window. All who saw this daunting spectacle spoke of how their eyes were drawn to the neck of the occupant of the coach and the tell-tale red ring which some held to be the sign of a beheading, others maintained it was clearly the mark of the hangman's noose.

Who was the man in the carriage? What had he done? What was the link with this place? The coach dates the man to a period between about 1600 and the coming of the railways two centuries later. During this time there is a record of just one crime in the area which would fit such a punishment, the murder of Gabriel Bigge.

It was 6 May 1615 and a quarrel had broken out between Bigge and labourer John Wybon. Wybon struck his victim a vicious and fatal blow on the head by a pike. Four days later Bigge was buried at nearby Norton Church. A tablet erected on the south wall of the church by his surviving family and friends described Bigge as *fortis et intrepidus* ('stronge and unshaken'). Thus he was probably at least as robust and hot-headed as his assailant – a factor which may well have contributed to his own death.

No record has been found of the fate of Wybon. Yet in an age when over 200 offences carried the death penalty – including the theft of a handkerchief – it is difficult to envisage anything but the gallows for him.

LEIGH

Old Colles

During the reign of Queen Elizabeth I the village of Leigh was home to Richard Colles, a justice of the peace who resided at Leigh Court. The story of Colles is similar to that of Lady Lightfoot at Shelsey Walsh (*see* page 99), although the conclusion is somewhat different.

Every year on the night of St Catherine's Eve, 24 November, the ghost known as Old Colles (or sometimes Old Coles) would return to the village of Leigh. His imminent return was announced by the tinkling of bells, whereupon a coach and jet black horses would be driven at a good pace through the village to his former home. The team, sometimes said to be four and sometimes twice that number, pulled the coach around the house thirteen times, no more and never less. On completion of the final circuit the whole ensemble would dash through the ancient tithe barn and into the River Teme beyond.

The reports had such an effect on the locals that a dozen of the local clergy decided to lay this tortured spirit to rest in a nearby pool through the power of the midnight bells, a book of prayers, and a candle. They allowed the candle to burn until just the final inch was left. Tossing the remaining lit stub into the pool they called upon Old Colles not to rise again until the candle was fully burned out. In order to ensure the candle was never relit they order the pool to be filled in.

Bell, book and candle are the traditional tools of exorcism and, while the tale may well be questionable, it seems to have had the desired result for there have been no reports of Old Colles for many years.

LITTLE MALVERN

The Dee Family

Walking into a pub late in the evening in the hope of finding a lead to a ghost story was not my usual method of research. Indeed it was only because I was staying overnight nearby, and had been engaged in conversation, that the topic had arisen at all. However, the sincerity of those who spoke to me that evening left a lasting impression and their stories are combined here.

I was told by several of the locals that the stories of the infamous Mr Dee had been passed down by word of mouth from generation to generation. For years the man had beaten his poor wife, however, in those days there was little chance of escape and she had to consider their daughter too. Eventually, either through ill health or the mistreatment she suffered due to his violent moods (and probably both), she lay dying. Almost with her dying breath she summoned the courage to warn him that unless he changed his ways and dismissed any ideas of cruelty to their daughter, she would return from the other side to exact her revenge.

At first the farm labourer controlled his temper; however, within months he was making his teenage daughter's life as miserable as he had her mother. The girl ran from the house, determined to throw herself in a nearby pond and free herself from her torment by drowning. However, the ghost of her mother was said to have risen from the cold waters, arms outstretched to prevent the girl from her intended suicide. So terrified was the girl at the sight before that she turned and ran back to the house she had just fled. However, when she returned she found her mother had carried out her threat and had wreaked havoc at her former home.

For months afterwards the woman is said to have appeared in many different places, revealing herself to labourers and their families. Eventually a priest was summoned to exorcise the spirit and, for a while at least, the spectre was not seen; whether this was due to the daughter leaving home or Mr Dee seeing the error of his ways is not known.

I was then told of how the distraught woman had seemingly returned to the Malverns. Within the last twenty years, as more and more people have walked this area of outstanding natural beauty, reports of a strange sight have filtered through. Sitting on a rock is the indistinct shape of a woman with her head bowed, as forlorn and miserable a figure as anyone could wish to see.

Dogs being walked here are said to act strangely and are reluctant to remain in the general area. When approached the figure dissolves into thin air. Locals maintain they have long known the area to be haunted and still advise the following generations to avoid that part of the Malverns.

If Mrs Dee has returned, we do not yet have any idea what her reasons are, or why she appears so saddened.

Hill Fort

Before the arrival of the Romans in AD 43, one of the major Briton settlements to have been founded in these islands was atop the Malverns, where a camp housing up to 4,000 individuals was occupied for four or five centuries. According to folklore, when the two cultures clashed it was here that the chieftain Caractacus was said to have retreated, to unite his forces at what he considered the most defensible position. He is said to have been captured and taken back to Rome to face the Emperor Claudius. Far from treating Caractacus as a prisoner, the emperor was so impressed that the Briton was given his own villa and nice pension to see out his days in comfort. (Modern historians now feel the last stronghold of the native Britons was at Church Stretton in Shropshire.)

However, folklore invariably has some basis in fact so perhaps the unwritten history is more accurate. If so, this would explain why, during the middle of the twentieth century, an entire column of Roman soldiers were seen marching up the Malvern slopes in full battle dress accompanied by standard bearers and cavalry. The eventual victors were seen to reach the summit and vanish.

MAMBLE

Sun and Slipper

The Sun and Slipper was first established in 1642 as a coaching inn and was originally known as just the Sun. The addition is thought to be a reference to a maintenance service offered on the coaches. During the twentieth century the name was changed to the Dog and Duck and later, through public pressure, changed back to its original name.

The present owners, Roger and his wife, moved in some fourteen years ago, taking over an establishment which had closed due to the previous owners running out of money. Some refurbishment was necessary to bring the place up to scratch before reopening and this seems to have been the catalyst for disturbing the resident ghost.

The apparition has never been seen by the owners, yet several customers have reported seeing a man of around 5ft 7in wearing the hairstyle and clothes of a seventeenth-century cavalier. A life-size artist's impression of the gentleman hangs in the dining room. It has been rumoured that this is the ghost of a man who was killed in a swordfight on the stairs in the pub. However, the stairs in question were not built until some considerable time later.

During the 1960s the then landlords called in a priest to conduct an exorcism when things became too much for them. It seems it must have been somewhat successful for nothing significant was reported until the present owners moved in.

As stated the place required some work prior to reopening. The major upheavals seem to disturb the resident ghost and almost instantly things started to happen. The first three nights that the pub was open again for business the door of the main bedroom opened and closed at exactly fifteen minutes after midnight. It cannot have blown open; the door is too heavy and would have had to move against gravity. Furthermore it did not slam shut but closed just as if being closed by someone. Since those first three nights there has been no repeat occurrence. However, the family's dogs refused to go anywhere near the living quarters upstairs for some time afterwards.

However, further unexplained phenomena continued. Classical music was heard playing in the kitchen for a few seconds, although there is no radio or other equipment in that vicinity. The bell, used to signal last orders, rang loud and clear for no apparent reason when nobody was close enough to ring it. There were also a number of occasions when glasses would fall from shelves without any obvious cause, and several people reported feeling a cold presence.

Approaching midnight on one occasion, Roger was in the cellar when he heard the sound of heavy footsteps above him, as if someone wearing boots was crossing the wooden floor in the bar overhead. As it was after closing, he thought a customer had somehow managed to get locked in and went upstairs to check. Yet there was nobody there and every door and window was still locked from the inside.

Every time the owners leave the premises for a holiday, the unexplained ghostly activity increases. Thus in 2004, when the Sun and Slipper underwent major refurbishment, both staff and regular customers were prepared for an increase in activity. Yet since that time there has not been a single sighting or any reports of any inexplicable activity.

Has the cavalier gone for good? It seems unlikely as he has been quiet for long periods before and the next major change is likely to be the signal for him to reappear once more.

MALVERN

Festival Theatre

In 1927 what had been the Assembly Rooms were purchased for the princely sum of £17,000 by the District Council. Two years later, following substantial alterations, the Festival Theatre opened its doors for the first time.

What began as a Drama Festival lasting a few days had, by 1934, expanded to a month. As other forms of entertainment competed for the audience the days of the annual festival, and even the theatre itself, were in doubt. During the period of uncertainty tireless work by volunteers and enthusiasts kept the theatre open. Changes in personnel brought new hope but little change in fortune. In 1950 the news came through of the death of George Bernard Shaw, the great Irish playwright who has forever been associated with the place. It must have seemed a bad omen for the theatre. In 1956 a celebration of the centenary of Shaw's birth saw a brief revival of interest.

It was around this time that unexplained and mysterious sounds seeming to emanate from the circle were reported. The sound of heavy footsteps echoed around the building in quieter times, while several people described a chill passing through them here. Backstage too, away from the public eye, doors banged shut when nobody was nearby and that same cold sensation was experienced.

Over the next twenty-five years several attempts were made to revive the Festival; however it was not until the emphasis returned to the works of George Bernard Shaw in 1977 that the corner was turned and the Festival Theatre saw a return to those more successful days once more.

The first presentation was *Man and Superman*, featuring the acting talents of Richard Pasco, Susan Hampshire and Nicky Henson. However, there was the feeling that not only the audience had returned.

As part of the rebirth in 1977, a number of valuable items were on loan to the theatre. The china and other personal items once owned by Shaw were stored in the cellar bar. An acquaintance of one of the volunteers was hired to act as night watchman, and although he had no previous experience he did have a large alsatian of fearsome appearance which made him the obvious choice. The dog and his master regularly patrolled the building to ensure all was well, yet the cellar was a place the canine would never enter. No amount of encouragement could make him proceed further than the top of the steps.

With audience figures swelling, particularly when one of Shaw's works was being performed, things were looking brighter for the first time in living memory. The Festival was once again an annual celebration and attracted more famous performers which, in turn, drew ever greater public interest, while the ghostly visitor also seemed to be drawn here, attracted by the theatre's revival.

It was during a performance of *You Never Can Tell* to a nearly full house that one performer was stunned to notice a familiar face seated in the circle. The full-bearded man stood out from the crowd, having a strangely white misty appearance. She was in no doubt this was the playwright himself, George Bernard Shaw.

For the next twenty years the reports continued, although never so frequently as during the late 1970s. They always centred on the circle and yet, when in attendance, Shaw was always seated in a box. Then, as the twentieth century drew to a close and the new millennium was dawning, the Festival Theatre saw a major refurbishment. The seating area and foyer were completely revamped and brought up to a standard befitting the twenty-first century. Since that time reports of anything from the newer areas have abruptly ceased.

However, backstage, where things have changed little for many years, the bumps and bangs, the chills and odd feelings continue. Does George Bernard Shaw, Malvern's

Malvern's theatres have been brought up to the twenty-first century, but retain an elegance.

very own adopted Irishman, still walk where he feels most at home, among the familiar areas of the theatre?

Warwick House

For over 170 years Warwick House was a major and prestigious department store. Self styled as the 'Top Peoples' Shop' it is, sadly, no more – having been converted into luxury apartments and houses.

Established as Cox and Painter in 1833, it later became Mitchell, Cox and Painter. The family retained the business for 145 years until 1978, when it was purchased by the Savile Row tailors of Gieves and Hawkes. Although all the customers have bought and paid for their last purchase some time ago, perhaps not every buyer has left the premises. Before the doors closed for the last time there were several reports of a memory from the time when it was the place to be seen by the cream of Victorian society in Malvern.

The children's department was one area where a lady was seen. She did not interact with any of the staff or customers; she just stood there as if waiting for someone or something. She was dressed in the style of a lady of some status from the Victorian age, wearing an ankle-length voluminous dress and a large hat. One assistant in the store refused to believe the stories of the ghostly lady's appearance, yet when the rota brought her to the children's department and she came face to face with the apparition she not only changed her mind but refused to ever work in that area ever again.

However, the assistant may not have escaped further confrontations by avoiding this floor, for the Victorian lady was also spotted elsewhere. She was regularly seen at the top of the stairs. Here she was referred to as the Lavender Lady on account of her perfume. She would be seen to travel along the passage of the upper floor and approach the stairs but not to descend them. The stairs were not installed in this part of the building until well into the twentieth century, which is why she ignores them and walks straight through the wall.

In order to satisfy the fears of some of the staff an exorcism was arranged. The manager brought in the local priest and the ceremony was initiated – however it was never completed. As the priest pointed out, exorcism was designed to rid places of malevolent ghosts or poltergeists. Whatever spirit was present in Warwick House, it was kind and friendly and added to the ambience of the place, so the exorcism was abandoned.

If the sightings were of one woman in several places, or of several women, and since the shop has closed we shall likely never know.

Mount Pleasant Hotel

Mount Pleasant Hotel is a Queen Anne building which affords great views over the picturesque Vale of Evesham and the Cotswolds, not forgetting the splendour of the

Mount Pleasant Hotel, Malvern.

adjacent priory. It was built for 'a princess' in 1730, with the new wing added in 1850, but in living memory was the home of Lloyds TSB.

Staff on the nightshift were concerned by the strange behaviour of the door to the store room. The room had only one door and no window and thus no draught, yet it regularly swung open of its own volition, seemingly defying the laws of physics.

Maybe the culprit is the grey hooded lady seen only at certain times of the year, presumably those same times as she visited Malvern during her life – perhaps to take the waters. One morning the coffee shop was unlocked for business in the morning and, much to the surprise of the key holder, a lady of the same description could be seen calmly seated at one of the tables. There was no sign of a forced entry and she certainly had not been there the previous evening when the shop was locked up for the night.

A lady answering the same description visited room number nine one night. The guest in that room awoke feeling cold and, as he looked toward the foot of the bed, saw the lady in the grey attire and wearing her hood simply standing there. Although she was looking in his general direction, he was adamant she was focused on something much further away, beyond the wall.

Despite so many sightings nobody has any idea who she might be or why she seems unable to find rest.

Lady Emily Foley

At the Foley Arms Hotel one finds its 200 years of history unfolding everywhere you look. Built in 1810 by Samuel Deykes, this Georgian coaching hotel built to accommodate the increasing numbers of visitors to Malvern as a spa town and to provide them with somewhere special to stay.

Today it remains an impressive and desirable establishment, but when it first opened it must have been one of the most elegant and exquisite hotels in the land. Magnificent bow windows afford unrivalled views of the landscape. Images of how it used to appear are found throughout the building. A clue to the hotel's popularity is the size and quality of the stables erected at the rear of the building.

The guest list also reveals the stature of the hotel. As you enter the building you cannot fail to see an impressive coat of arms. This was presented to the hotel during the six-week stay by Princess Mary of Teck, later queen consort of George V and the grandmother of Queen Elizabeth II. Photographs of the princess in her younger days stand alongside a portrait of Lady Emily Foley, the subject of our story.

As her name suggests, Lady Foley was a descendant of the family who owned much of Malvern, including the hotel. She was the Lady of the Manor of Malvern during the Victorian era and would arrive at her hotel every August from her country seat at Stoke Edith Park. Nobody would have been unaware of her arrival from the moment her huge horse-drawn carriage arrived in the town, accompanied by her coach men in their livery of red and yellow. Many artefacts are displayed throughout the hotel to commemorate her visits. Her ladyship was renowned as a formidable woman and all local dignitaries were expected to pay their respects during her annual visit.

*The impressive façade of
Foley Arms Hotel, Malvern.*

Woe betide those who failed to be checked off the list, for her displeasure would be made known vociferously. It was said that grown men would tremble at the thought of incurring the wrath of the Lady Emily.

Whilst she may have been a frightening figure, exacting the same demanding standard from everyone and everything she encountered as she set for herself, she was also a generous and supportive member of her ancestral manor. So it was a sad day when it was learned of her passing at the stroke of midnight on 31 December 1899.

Yet while her visits to the hotel were limited to her annual late summer trip in life, since her death she has been in permanent residence. Both staff and knowledgeable guests have encountered her presence in the corridors of the hotel, while others have heard the rustling of her dresses as she checks that all is well. Of course she would never deign to enter any of the rooms themselves; the privacy of the guests was a primary consideration. She has also been sensed in the cellars below the hotel. These are quite extensive, stretching out to below the level of the road itself, so as to allow deliveries to be made without interfering with the guests as much as to provide extra storage space.

Her portrait keeps watch on those who enter and leave her beloved hotel, a palpable presence somehow still commanding respect, while she herself keeps an eye on events behind the scenes. Yet all agree that, while she may have been a terrifying figure in her lifetime, her ghost is as friendly as any they would hope to encounter.

Nicholson Organs

Nicholson Organs was a company founded in 1841 by John Nicholson to manufacture pipe organs. Their reputation of building quality instruments has lead to Nicholson Organs being found in Malvern Priory, Gloucester Cathedral, Southwell Minster, and Portsmouth Cathedral amongst others. Each organ is produced with the building in which it will be housed in mind, producing the ideal tonal quality.

In 2003 the factory was relocated to Leigh Sinton from its site in Quest Hills Road, a former vet's practice which it had occupied for over a century. At Malvern the facilities at the vet's provided stabling for the company's horses, the only form of power until the 1930s when coal was readily available and then electricity in the 1950s. Organs were produced in a factory located in the unlikely setting of an assemblage of quaint old buildings, with a well pumped by hand, yet somehow it worked.

It was at Quest Hills Road that the staff, who often came into work early or during the quieter periods at the weekend, reported an unseen visitor walking about. Footsteps were heard ascending the old wooden stairs and across what used to be the hayloft. Reports suggested it sounded just as if it was an echo, a memory of a former stable hand moving hay bales to feed the animals.

The former factory has now been redeveloped as a number of new homes, tastefully styled to fit its earlier appearance. But has the stable boy moved with the business to its new home at Leigh Sinton or does he remain in Quest Hills Road.

Great Malvern Priory

The Benedictine monastery of Great Malvern Priory (c. 1075–1540) was traditionally founded by a hermit called Aldwyn at the request of St Wulfstan, then the Bishop of Worcester. It exhibits a fine collection of stained glass dating from the fifteenth century up to the present day and was expertly restored in the 1860s by the architect Sir George Gilbert Scott.

As with many old churches it takes a good deal of money to maintain the building and this church, like many others, has a bookshop. Next to this bookshop is a small room, one of those places referred to as a store cupboard but ostensibly a repository for anything unwanted.

In the years before the bookshop this area was laid out rather differently, which may be the reason why a young girl seems to be oblivious of the presence of the new fittings and walks straight through them. She appears wearing the clothes of a young peasant girl, no older than ten, making dating difficult. Others have witnessed her entering through the closed doors of the porch as if they were still wide open.

In another part of the priory is St Anne's Chapel, created to be a region for quiet prayer and reflection; a monk has been sighted here several times. He is always seen on the move, never in prayer, and surprisingly all reports centre on his broad and highly exaggerated smile. Unlike the girl he seems fully aware of his modern surroundings, even making eye contact with some witnesses.

No suggestions have been offered as to the identity of either apparitions, and a visit to Great Malvern Priory for an interview failed to see the subjects materialise.

Abbey Hotel

Situated near the Abbey, this Victorian hotel is hidden behind a front of Virginia creeper, a quite magnificent sight in its brilliant red hue in the autumn. The hotel was built when Malvern was a Mecca for the Victorians seeking its medicinal spa waters and continues to accommodate guests in the greatest comfort.

The Abbey, which gave it its name, is adjacent to the hotel in Abbey Road. Built in the middle of the nineteenth century, the hotel has two non-paying guests – a monk and a nun. Whilst the monk could be a memory from the Benedictine monastery, there is no history of any nuns being resident there.

Staff have noted several occasions when their presence has been sensed, yet there is no feeling of animosity. There is also no reason to suppose the two are in any way linked as they have never been witnessed at the same time. However it does make one wonder if either spirit is aware of, or interacts with, the other.

MIDDLE LITTLETON

Hide and Seek

On a warm summer evening a cool refreshing drink and friendly conversation is most enjoyable, especially in the countryside when the kids can be allowed to run free and play. Such was the case when an extended family had gathered in Middle Littleton, the parents of the three children were brothers and sisters and had grown up around the area and so knew it well. This particular evening the adults were sipping something cool after a hard day, or so they maintained, while the cousins were burning off excess energy by indulging in the ageless game of hide and seek in and around the quiet village.

After the eldest had gone off to hide, the two girls counted the required number before setting off in search of him. They ran off down a narrow footpath which led towards the churchyard and, as they rounded a corner, screamed and ran back to their parents. As they caught their breath they described what they had seen – two rows of girls, five in each row with one standing and those at the front kneeling, on the path in front of them. They were all of a strangely grey appearance, with long hair and wearing what appeared to be night attire.

As the grown-ups dismissed their story and told them to 'go and play', they returned to see what had become of their cousin. They found him and pointed out where they had seen the strange girls, yet he had seen nothing. However, he did say he had heard a man shouting, the voice sounded angry and had an oddly echoing sound to it, but he had seen no girls.

No explanation or link to the past has ever been suggested for this sighting and it appears to be the only reported incident of this nature here.

NORTH LITTLETON

Home Sweet Home

This story is a little different, for most involve a ghost being stirred by new activity. While this is somewhat true to start with, ultimately though, we find the reverse seems to be the case.

In the early days of a young family one of the most exciting days is that time when feet are firmly on the property ladder and finances allow for a move to a new home. Not just a move to a bigger property, but a little luxury, a more desirable area, or that dream cottage. It was just such circumstances which allowed a young family of four to move to an old house in North Littleton. The place required some considerable work being done before they could move in and their alterations seemed to have disturbed the resident ghost.

During those first months the main door seemed to be the focus for the attention. Several times they saw the old-style latch lift and the door open without anyone there. Furthermore it was not only the family who witnessed this, when the babysitter was looking after their two pre-school boys she watched open-mouthed as the latch moved and the door slowly open. It should be noted that the balance of the door would make it close when it was left alone and was too heavy to be moved by anything but the strongest breeze. Items also started being moved. Ornaments and trinkets on shelves, in cupboards and even on top of the television set were moved. He blamed her, she blamed him and eventually, as the children were unable to reach, they conceded the culprit was their unseen resident. Yet he did not stay unseen.

Being an old property they did not have an upstairs bathroom and thus, in order to answer a call of nature during the night, they were forced to descend the stairs. Some years after they had first moved in their youngest awoke for just this reason and had started to walk down the stairs when he noticed a figure standing in the doorway to the bathroom that was clearly not going to let him pass. The youngster called out to his parents and father responded forcefully. His voice, amplified by the solid surfaces of the bathroom, boomed out a warning: 'Haunt all you desire but interfere with my children and the house will be in flames before you know it, leaving you homeless!' This had an almost instant calming effect and little trouble was had from their unseen visitor.

Although the family had always tried to maintain the original layout of the building as much as possible, this eventually proved impossible. As with boys of all ages, thoughts eventually turned to a model train set and the time came when a layout was imperative. With space at a premium, it was decided to create a loft in the beams and floorboards were installed and a carpet laid to provide some comfort. From that moment on not a sign of the ghostly visitor was ever heard, seen or felt again.

Had the new construction in the roof, so often the catalyst for the resident haunting to manifest itself, this time laid the individual to rest?

PEDMORE

Wychbury Hill

An ancient hill fort stands just below the summit of the 220m-high Wychbury Hill. This is by no means one of the oldest of the fortified hill forts of pre-Roman occupation, nor is it the largest; however, if some of the reports are accurate, it is the only one still playing host to its early occupants.

While the general understanding of the arrival of the Romans in AD 43 is one of conflict and battles, this has been based on the written record left to us by the conquerors and does not quite tell the whole story. Britain had traded with the Empire for many years before the legions arrived. Indeed they had had little choice as the rest of the known world, from their perspective, was under Roman rule. It is now accepted that many tribes of Britons were largely responsible for inviting the Empire to our lands, albeit they probably had little choice. Hence the legions arrived and, without united opposition, soon had control with just isolated pockets of stubborn resistance.

This Worcestershire hill fort was one of those places which saw fighting between the native Britons and the Romans. The memory of this conflict has been heard echoing around the slopes of the prominent hill; sounds of battle, of metal clashing, the barked orders of the commanders, the screams and moans of the casualties. There have also been sightings of one solitary Roman soldier. He stands, unmoving, within the walls of the fortification. Perhaps he is surveying the carnage only he can see, reflecting upon the suffering, grieving for his fallen comrades and honouring the bravery of the enemy. Before long he fades from sight.

Is he the ghost of one of the fallen, or perhaps the spirit of one who survived and is kept here by the sadness and despair of what he has witnessed? He has been sighted a number of times over the last two centuries, each being a brief but poignant appearance.

PERSHORE

A Screaming Phantom

The eleventh-century Pershore Abbey has seen several major repairs and rebuilding programmes over the centuries. During this time there have been numerous reports of an awful noise emanating from this ancient place of worship. Nothing is ever reported as being seen, however this is not surprising for none would dare to enter the building when a phantom's scream was echoing around the place. At this time locals who lived within earshot were so terrorised by the noise they refused to leave their homes.

Some 300m north-east of the Abbey in High Street is the Pershore Working Men's Club. In the latter half of the twentieth century a number of members, and their guests, reported seeing an ominous shadowy figure entering the building and making for the concert room. This was an unwelcome spirit, repeatedly breaking glasses and damaging fixtures and fittings. The problem resulted in the police being called and an investigation ensued, which revealed nothing untoward.

When the subject of ghosts is broached there are always sceptics. One such Pershore man dismissed the High Street club's so-called ghost as a figment of several over-active imaginations and volunteered to spend the night on the premises. He failed, fleeing the building within a couple of hours, overwhelmed by a terrifying sense of utter dread.

Angel Inn & Posting House

A visit to the Angel Inn & Posting House, an utterly charming establishment, proved well worth the time. The most friendly welcome was afforded by the manager Juan

The Angel Inn & Posting House must have been a grand stop on the old coaching routes.

Mendez. I had dropped in to hear about a ghostly sailor and learned there was more to this story than I had ever expected.

Since the 1990s a number of customers have said they felt a presence in the lounge, the bars and in the restaurant. On different occasions a man described as a sailor, wearing a dark blue donkey jacket over what appeared to be a uniform of the Royal Navy dating from around the end of the Second World War has been seen standing in front of the fireplace in the restaurant. Thus it may not be the same person whose presence is felt elsewhere. Is he the memory of a soldier who failed to come home to his family?

Mr Mendez also informed me how, for some time prior to my visit, unexplained noises had been heard coming from closed rooms which were found to be empty. It was while he and his staff were discussing these events after the customers had gone home one evening when the most worrying event occurred. It was approaching 1 a.m. and they were gathered in the lounge. As with many inns throughout the land, the walls are adorned by decorative plates. It was one of these plates which, to the great consternation of the staff in the middle of their ghostly conversation, suddenly shattered into a thousand pieces. As Juan Mendez explained, 'the plate did not fall from the wall and break, it quite literally exploded where it hung on the wall as if hit very hard.'

Did the ghost here wish to comment on their conversation about his possible presence by getting their attention? If so, it most certainly worked.

River Avon

It was August 1965 and the greatest season in the history of English football was about to kick off, yet victory in the World Cup the following summer was far from the minds of a veritable army of ghost hunters who descended on Pershore.

For a whole week they suffered sleepless nights in the late summer, snatching what sleep they could in the heat of the day. However, their efforts did not go unrewarded for during that week several strange entities were seen, mostly in the distance, yet there were some undoubtedly spectacular results. They worked on the premise that the busiest areas would harbour the most ghosts; this would logically be the bridge into the town across the Avon. On one night several witnessed a strange glowing square which lay flat in the meadow alongside the river, although no explanation as to what it represented was offered. This was followed later in the week by a 6ft figure walking off towards the churchyard about 3ft above the level of the ground. Was the figure following the level of the land as it would have been when that person was still alive?

However, the most impressive report was when fifty of those present surrounded a misty form near the bridge. They formed a circle around it and, seconds later, it vanished. None of them could make out any recognisable form in the mist, there was no suggestion that it had human form, and after that nothing more was seen for the rest of the week.

THE PORTWAY

Molly Moor

North of Redditch on the road to Alcester is The Portway. There is a distinct rise here which was the site of a hangman's gallows where eight individuals were hanged for their crimes many centuries ago. On that same site cottages were built and in the late seventeenth century our story began to unfold.

A labourer resided here by the name of Hunt. He became the target of ridicule from his colleagues, Bishop, Carr and Edwards, for claiming his home was haunted. Hunt fought back and dared them to stay at his home for a whole night. Not only did they accept the challenge but Edwards promised, should she appear, he would give Molly – the resident ghost –a big kiss.

On the night in question the three men arrived with much scepticism and a large bottle of ale. As midnight approached footsteps were heard overhead. They crossed the floorboards and were heard descending the stairs. Edwards, suspecting a hoax, leapt from his seat and ran to greet 'Molly' at the bottom step and give her the kiss he had promised. Several loud crashes rang out and then total silence.

Next morning the three burly men were found unconscious amidst a scene of broken crockery and scattered household items. Despite offers no amount of money could encourage the three men to spend another night in the cottage.

A little detective work 100 years after the event revealed that, among the eight hanged, was one by the name of Moor. The Christian name is not recorded, however if Moor was really a Molly, then she must have been a formidable opponent to see off three strong men alone.

REDDITCH

Moons Moat

The name Moons Moat will not be lost on those familiar with the town. It adorns both a road and the nearby industrial estate. However, the history of the name dates back to at least the sixteenth century.

Moons Moat was a medieval moated settlement, now a part of the Church Hill housing estate. Originally it was a hunting lodge, protected by a moat. This moat was later extended to form a fishing pond. Today the land is overgrown and is an eyesore, only the moat remains and that is now dry. However, there has been a major drive to fence the area off, to clean it up and eventually revive a piece of history.

Every year on 20 January a woman in medieval attire is said to roam this small historical site. This date is the eve of the feast of St Agnes, however it is unknown if this is of any significance. The name of the place is a corruption of Mohun, the name of the family who owned the house. Hence the name given to the woman who appears here is Lady Mohun. It will be interesting to see if her appearance is affected by the renovation.

Dog & Pheasant

Today the Dog & Pheasant is regarded as an old public house, however the building was standing long before it was a licensed premises. This charming traditional pub has two reported apparitions. One is content to roam with the customers; the other is more interested in operations behind the scenes.

Landlady Myrna has been here since the start of the twenty-first century. Her experiences are limited to one sighting. It was shortly after her arrival and, as we all do, she desired to give her new home a good clean. Good stocks of cleaning materials were brought in and stored on a shelf in a cupboard. Within moments a noise was heard and, upon investigation, found to be on the floor of the small cupboard without any rational explanation as to how they had fallen. Fortunately all were intact.

The same cupboard continues to house the cleaning equipment today. However, when Myrna opened the door one evening at around eight, she found more than she expected. A boy of about ten was crouching down as if hiding. He was wearing jodhpurs, a woollen jumper and a flat cap, in a style akin to the Edwardian era. Before

The Dog & Pheasant at Redditch.

she had time to say a word he had fled, leaving her with a distinctly peculiar feeling. Although he has not been seen since, she has sensed his presence by the same truly odd feeling.

The other individual is an old woman who has been seen by others, but never by Myrna. Indeed one evening Maggie, a friend of the licensee, pointed the woman out when she was sitting in her favoured seat by the door. Myrna looked but could not see anyone. As they stood she was seen to rise and walk straight through a wood and glass partition as if it did not exist. Several people have witnessed the woman at different times, while customers and staff in the room at the same time have seen nothing. She has also been blamed for rolling bottles across the floor in the bar.

There is a theory that she is a former resident of the place and her antics are simply those of a house-proud individual tidying up her home. Maybe the young boy was a relative of hers and also lived in the place when it was a home.

Hewell Grange

As the manor house of the Earl of Plymouth, Hewell Grange has historical associations with nearby Bordesley Abbey. In February 2001 the monks and the estate of the Windsor family were spoken of for the first time in many, many years.

Towards the end of the nineteenth century an impressive three-storey mansion was constructed. Overlooking the delightful gardens, it was a home for only fifty years before being utilised as a borstal from 1946, a youth custody centre from 1988, and in the 1990s a female prison. At the beginning of the twenty-first century it housed 159 female inmates and staff, having changed its name to Brockhill.

In 2001 reports began to filter out of the prison of a male visitor who was turning up outside visiting times. In one particular area of Brockhill several prisoners claimed to have seen a monk wearing the distinctive habit of these men of God. Appearing late into the evening he was observed walking through the cells, passing through the walls from one room to the next. Staff had told of the weird sensations felt while on nightshift duty in this part of the building. A cold presence caused the hairs on the back of the neck to stand up and they were convinced they were not alone.

With no other known sightings, ghost hunters were perplexed by the monk's sudden appearance. However, a possible reason was discovered during a routine search of the cells when the remains of a home-made Ouija board was found. Was it that the reports of the ghost had disturbed the experimenters to the point where they had felt it necessary to destroy the evidence, or are the two unrelated?

Being unable to escape their uninvited visitor, the inmates were understandably frightened. Staff were also said to dread the nightshift. Support was available, either in the form of spiritual guidance by the prison chaplain or counselling by trained professionals, and had been offered to any who felt they needed it.

However, not everyone was as concerned. An alleged comment by one of the women prisoners showed how some saw the problem in a quite different light: 'What luck! A man visiting our cells late at night and he's a monk. Not much good to us!'

Bordesley Abbey

The monk of Hewell Grange (*see* previous story) was said to be from Bordesley Abbey, a logical deduction considering they shared the same estate at various times. The Abbey was founded in 1140 by Cistercian monks from Garendon Abbey, in Leicestershire, on lands granted by Waleran de Beaumont, the Count of Meulan and the Earl of Worcester.

Such generosity was not without its problems. The valley was unproductive marshland, an impossible site on which to build a large Abbey. Unperturbed the monks dug a complex yet efficient drainage system, effectively diverting the River Arrow. Early buildings were of wood, but were replaced with stone within a few short years. Over the next four centuries the Abbey grew in wealth, largely through the sale of cereals and wool, produce from its twenty farms. It all came crashing down in 1538, when Henry VIII dissolved the monasteries as part of his break from the Catholic Church.

The work of the monks, while undoubtedly beneficial to Redditch, is said to have awoken an ancient denizen of this valley. England has more reports of ghostly black dogs than anywhere in the world, each region having its own terminology (*see* Bredon). It is said that only the steadfast faith of the monks prevented the fearsome animal from reclaiming its territory. Something it later achieved – with a little help from King Henry.

It is said there is no smoke without fire, that all folklore has some basis in historical fact. For once we may know the origins of this narrative. Edward I's reign was a turbulent one, perhaps fuelled by his displeasure of his heir's relationship with Piers Gaveston. The King elicited a solemn oath from his son that he would end the friendship and, as a result, came to the throne upon the death of his father. However, he reneged on his promise and showered Gaveston with titles, lands and wealth, much to the displeasure of the nobility and the Church.

One man who was particularly displeased was Guy de Beauchamp, Earl of Warwick. As Edward II's power ebbed away Gaveston's influence waned and he fled the country. Upon his return the Earl of Warwick organised his capture and he was beheaded at Blacklow Hill; dragged there kicking and screaming, his end was an undignified one. As Gaveston faced his enemy for the final time, Warwick is said to have grinned and said, 'The Black Dog of Arden has come to keep the oath he swore, that you should one day feel his teeth.'

It was Gaveston himself who had styled Warwick the 'Black Dog of Arden' on account of his dark complexion.

Old Rectory Hotel

The Old Rectory Hotel is a building with a long and changing history. A delightful property set in four acres of wooded gardens between the Roman road of Ickneild Street and the carp lakes which fed the monks. An architectural facelift in 1812 brought about the Georgian façade we see today. This was a task engineered by a man of an incomparable lineage in such matter, the great-grandson of Sir Christopher Wren who lived here for over forty years.

With such a lengthy heritage it would not seem fitting if there were not at least one story of a former resident to tell; indeed there are several. A psychic expert who visited the hotel spoke of a young woman, a resident of this area during the Roman occupation. She is said to have met a tragic end, hence she continues to roam here, dressed in white. On another occasion there was a report of a woman seated in a large chair in the lounge. She had extraordinarily dark eyes and an unnerving stare. A dog has been felt to brush past the legs in this same room and in the connecting corridor. Electric kettles have been known to switch on without anyone near, lights too, and other objects apparently move of their own volition and doors close suddenly without apparent cause.

However, the most enduring tale is that of the priest. He has been seen at a first-floor bedroom window, gazing out across the estate. One neighbour maintains there is a photograph of such an occurrence, showing an odd blurring at this one window. This room, number four and the former chapel of the rectory, is a large room with a barrel ceiling. Several times over the years visitors have reported an inexplicable chill which, oddly, always occurs at 4 a.m.

A traditional tale is told hereabouts of a pious man, a kind and caring individual whose life was enriched by his lovely wife and their two daughters. Things changed when the lady of the house was taken seriously ill. After a short time she succumbed to the disease, leaving the man a grief-stricken widower. However, further tragedy was

The Old Rectory Hotel, Ipsley, Redditch.

to befall the family, for soon afterwards both daughters were also struck by the same symptoms and they too were soon dead.

The loss of his family drove the man into a state of utter despair. He laid both daughters out in the chapel, visiting them often and weeping pitifully as he sat with them, stroking their hair. Initially he refused to allow them to be buried and continued to mourn their passing most audibly. Eventually he relented and they were finally laid to rest. He continued to mourn the loss of his beloved family for the rest of his life.

Those who have been awoken by the cold chill in room number four, have also said they have felt a hand stroking the hair on their head.

The Redcoat

The Redcoat is a popular pub on the Studley road which has had a visitor in the past, although neither the current staff nor management have seen any sign of the individual in question.

During the twentieth century there had been a number of second-hand reports of a gentleman from the past walking along the bar top. It seems he wore the attire of a British soldier from the eighteenth century, as would have been worn during the American War of Independence when they were described as Redcoats – for obvious reasons.

Unusually, the soldier seemed to be aware of his surroundings and paraded along the bar top seemingly having had a little too much to drink. His visits were short but entertaining – however, nobody has ever discussed whether he is intoxicated by a brew from his time or from the modern era.

John the Gardener

This story comes from a time when surnames were unusual, a time when a point of origin or (as here) a trade were all that was needed to identify the individual. As with modern surnames the trade was passed on to their descendants and served as a family name for some time.

John lived in a cottage and seemingly continued to do so after his death. After his death the cottage remained empty, although whether this was because of John's ghost is unrecorded. During the day he was blamed for moving a number of items, not removing them but relocating them. However, his practical jokes did not satisfy him at night and so, irritated by everyone sleeping while he was still wide awake, he was off on his rounds in the early hours. Incidentally, to the author's knowledge there has never been a report of a ghost sleeping – which raises the question as to whether these spirits require sleep?

So John, who should probably be referred to as a former gardener, did everything he could to spoil the sleep of the villagers. One woman complained that he would raise the most raucous of sounds, once seemingly dropping a full cart-load of gravel on her roof. Occasionally he was seen – always appearing as an animal. He was easily recognised, for, no matter what creature he became, it was always a ghostly white. One couple recognised him instantly, even though the creature moved so rapidly they were unable to identify what form he had assumed. Sitting on a bench the young sweethearts had been talking – about whatever courting couples found to talk about in those days – when the white beastly form shot right between them (note the discreet gap). They fled their separate ways, she indoors and he off to his home.

Fortunately, the experience did not have a lasting negative effect on the romance. They were married soon afterwards and remained husband and wife for the rest of their lives.

Fish Hill

Redditch is justifiably proud of its history of needle manufacture, as evidenced by the Forge Mill Needle Museum. The museum occupies the premises of British Needle Mills, which in turn stood on the site of two or three cottages.

It was into one of these cottages that a young married couple moved. On the first night in their home they were seriously considering the wisdom of their choice of home. With the good lady already tucked in, her husband climbed the stairs and prepared for bed. He gave a cursory glance around the room before blowing out the candle and noticed the bedroom door was wide open. Although he was fairly sure he could remember dropping the latch on the door the first time, he got up and closed the door firmly. This time when he got into bed he was stunned to see the door wide open once more.

Once more he roused himself and closed the door, nipping back to blow out the candle and yet, even in the darkness, his wife could see the door was once again wide open. One last time he latched the door and, backing away towards their bed, watched as the door slowly opened. Night after night this occurred; rarely would the door remain closed for more than a few seconds.

One day the culprit was discovered. A loose floorboard and an ill-fitting latch combined to open the door every time the floorboard was stepped on. A few nails later and the 'exorcism' was complete.

Lily Green

This ghost is not that of a woman, despite the name and the folklore, but is named after a farm. It seems the gentleman in question is a restless soul and has tested the resolve of many over the years.

No identity has ever been suggested. Not even by the half dozen or so clergymen who finally managed to lay his spirit to rest at the bottom of the pond next to the farmhouse. However, over time the pond silted up and he was released. Quite soon afterwards reports of his return were recorded from the Headless Cross area.

One resident reported how he was, 'heard to be planing and sawing, as if making a coffin', but each time he ascended the stairs of the old farmhouse to investigate further the sounds would abruptly cease. By the time he reached the room and opened the door there was nobody there and no sign of any woodworking activity whatsoever.

A gate on the farm has also attracted attention. Several farmworkers over the centuries have stated how difficult it has been to drive horses and cattle through it. Their terror was such that they would be 'brought to a foam' and 'quivering in every limb'. The gate adjoins a wall, where one man reported seeing a hand extend out from the stonework, revealing a 'ruffled sleeve'.

The description of the clothing on the disembodied arm suggests a wealthier person than the phantom carpenter from the farmhouse. Therefore it is likely there are two quite separate ghostly visitors here.

Ghostly Hill

Forget the image of a large prominent hill, to the Saxons who first named Ghostly Hill any rise in this generally flat area was a hill. It was on that 'hill' that a charcoal burner worked. His task was among the most tedious in the days before coal was mined.

Cut wood was stacked in such a way that, when it was covered with earth and lit, being starved of much oxygen the wood only smouldered. This rid it of water and other volatile ingredients, making it burn with a much cleaner flame. However, the fire had to be watched continuously, sometimes for days, so the fire did not go out nor did it go up in flames. The charcoal burner sat on a stool with just one leg as he watched, for this way if he did go to sleep he would fall. This is the origin of the phrase 'to drop off to sleep'.

However, one charcoal burner did fall asleep and was asphyxiated by the fumes from the charcoal pile. In later years it was said you could still hear the crackling of the burning thorn bushes, warning of the return of the old man.

It is not only a phantom charcoal burner that has been seen here. William Guardner was walking across the field when he spotted a familiar figure ahead of him. He soon realised what he was seeing was a duplicate of himself, wearing clothes which he thought were hanging in his own wardrobe.

Visibly shaken he chased after the figure, yet, no matter how hard he tried, he could not close the gap even though his other self never hurried. On reaching the stile at the lane the doppelganger promptly vanished. William was fearful; such a sight (also known as a fetch) was considered an omen of the most awful kind.

However, he returned to his daily work and, one week later, fell from a hay rick in this very same field and was killed outright.

Snow Trouble

During the latter half of the 1970s a cold front had brought a blast of cold air down from Scandinavia and had hit the warmer wet air of the Gulf Stream. The resulting snowfall had blanketed the countryside of north Worcestershire and, although the roads had been cleared by passage of traffic, the overnight drop in temperature had produced a skating rink where the tarmac on the outskirts of Redditch had once been.

The treacherous conditions caught one driver out that morning. Despite being an experienced motorist, using his gears to regulate his speed and little more than crawling along the virtually empty roads, a right-hand bend proved too much and he found himself off the road in a hedge. Unable to reverse he climbed out to inspect the damage and, circling the vehicle, found the hedge and ditch had trapped him and the chances of getting any traction with his car's front wheel drive seemed remote. His red car was stuck with its front wheels over the ditch in front of the hedge, although it was difficult to tell with the thick and undisturbed blanket of snow. The white covering also hid anything which he may have been able to place under the wheels in order to get a grip and back out.

Getting back into his vehicle he restarted the engine and put it into reverse to give a token second try when he suddenly spotted an old woman. The woman, wearing a shapeless cloak or habit, seemed to pass a hand lightly over the car and instantly disappear. She had appeared to float, to swing round as if suspended from above, moving far too easily over ground which was so thick with snow it was hard to put one foot in front of the other effortlessly. In his shock and ensuing state of panic the man reversed back on to the road and continued his journey before he realised he had just escaped from a position which, moments earlier, he had been resigned to being stuck in.

Later he recounted the story to a friend who told him that area had been the site of an old convent.

Door Trouble

A door is among the simplest of devices for all it does is open and close – or does it? At one cycle sales and repair shop in Redditch things were never that simple with one particular door.

On occasions the door refused to open to customers, even though it was unlocked and simply on the ball catch. This was not good, for customers often walked away believing the place was closed. Conversely on one occassion when the owner was out of the shop and across the road, keeping an eye out for potential custom, he was suddenly aware of the door being ajar when he knew he had closed it to keep the heat in. Although he had not noticed anyone enter his premises he rushed across to attend to the customer – but when he arrived there was nobody there.

Eventually the poor man started to believe he was imagining everything. Until one day he was in the rear of the shop with a representative from a supplier. The visitor was well acquainted with the mysterious door and was sceptical at any suggestion of a ghostly culprit. When they heard the door open they both turned to see who had entered the shop and was surprised to find nobody there. After that experience the sales rep was less scathing in his remarks.

Kingfisher Centre

One of the best-known shopping centres in the Midlands, the Kingfisher Centre, has attracted visitors from far and near. One paricular couple have been reported as coming from very close to home although, as far as anyone knows, have yet to spend a single penny here.

At the tip of the region covered by this large modern construction there is a much earlier church. The church still stands, albeit dwarfed by its vast, modern neighbour. It has long been thought that the building of the Kingfisher Centre encroached upon part of the graveyard of the church. This was given as the reason why there had been sightings of two ghostly individuals, who are believed to be a man and a woman whose graves had been disturbed by the development of the twentieth century.

The male is said to be a monk. Always seen cowled and with his face hidden, he keeps to the shadows and never interacts with anyone. However, the woman, elderly with drab worn clothing, seems puzzled or lost. Confused by her surroundings she takes little notice of passers-by but seems aware of the mass of concrete and the buildings.

It remains to be seen if they are associated with the graveyard. Yet it should be noted that there is no evidence of disturbance of any graves during construction and this is probably something which has developed to explain the sightings rather than the reverse. The sightings of the monk would, on the face of it, suggest this individual was not buried in the local graveyard. His attire does not help to date him at all, yet we would certainly not expect to find him interred in a parish church. Conversely, the description of the woman seems to correlate with the dates and eras pertaining to those in the graveyard.

SALWARPE

A Drowning Ghost

The Droitwich Canal was simply a parallel cutting to the River Salwarpe, made navigable in the 1660s by the addition of a few locks. Despite what some historians have suggested, there is no reason to suppose it was built to transport salt out, more likely to bring coal in. Whatever its purpose, Andrew Yarranton's design was abandoned five years later, before completion.

While the work continued a side of the half-timbered old manor building which stood here was sliced away. It seems this must have been a mistake; the most likely explanation being that the foundations were weakened by the work and the side of the building fell away. At the time the occupant was understandably irritated, but not as much as a former owner who apparently returned to his home to seek revenge on those who had defaced his favourite abode.

From that time he was said to have appeared before the servants of the house, scaring them half to death. Furthermore he was also said to have attempted to frighten off the workmen. Often he was seen to glide down towards the river and throw himself into the depths of the waters in a ritualistic suicide.

That the work continued well past the manor house almost to meet the Severn may seem to suggest the attempt failed. Yet if we were to look at it from another angle perhaps the project was abandoned because of the haunting. However, as the ghost is only recorded during the hours of darkness, when the work had ceased, it seems there must have been a different reason for the canal being unfinished.

SHELSEY WALSH
Ghostly Coach

Sometimes referred to as Little Shelsey, the old courthouse here had been the site of some strange occurrences up to the middle of the twentieth century.

It was here during the sixteenth century that Lady Lightfoot was held prisoner. Whilst today the tabloids produce an endless stream of criticism of even the smallest *faux pas* by the monarchy, in the sixteenth century the lady's outspoken views of Henry VIII and his succession of marriages led to her arrest and imprisonment.

There is a record of a rescue attempt, made while the house was distracted by Christmas celebrations and festivities. The rescue party arrived in a coach and horses, but chose to use a drunken driver who was unable to control the horses. When the animals bolted he lost control, and horses, coach and would-be rescuers ended up in the moat where they drowned. Their attempts would have been in vain anyway for the Lady Lightfoot was already dead, murdered by those who had detained her.

The ghost of Lady Lightfoot has been seen to drive up to the house in the coach of her rescuers. Circling the property, the horses are then turned directly toward it and the whole ensemble passes straight through the solid building accompanied by the most awful screams. Some reports state they end up, once again, in the moat. The ghostly coach is swallowed up entirely by the waters, leaving only bubbles of acrid smoke coming to the surface. Visitors to the house have also complained of hearing the most unearthly screams from somewhere within.

It does seem rather unusual that the victim and not the perpetrators of the crime has not been allowed to rest in peace. Indeed, why she should appear in the coach when she never even saw it is also rather odd. Maybe her desire for revenge has brought her eternal misery, much as her refusal to keep silent landed her in trouble in the first place.

SOUTH LITTLETON

Unseen Road

At some point during the nineteenth century the road from here to Bretforton was redirected. This tale is of particular interest as it has remarkable similarities with the author's single, split-second experience mentioned in the Introduction.

The route of the road needed to be altered because of the railway; however, the apparition has never been seen near the single trackway here but where the road used to run to the east of its present path. It is along this old road that a coach and four are seen travelling, a road which no longer exists and has been ploughed many times, and planted with a series of dividing hedgerows and copses. Such a surface could hardly afford the smoothest of rides, no matter how good the suspension. Yet the horses do not stumble or break stride, while the coach glides smoothly across a terrain it could never have crossed in reality. Historically no coach has ever been known to have used this route and at night, with only a ghostly form to gauge by, it is difficult to see if this is a private vehicle.

As mentioned there is a great similarity here with the author's only unexplained experience. It was around 10 p.m. on an autumn evening on a familiar unlit road. Rounding a curve the car's headlights illuminated a line of mist at the bottom of the slope and a coach and four travelling through the mist. Following a little research it was discovered no coach route ever crossed this road and furthermore, and this is where the stories differ, there was never a road here either during the days of coaching or as far back as the Roman occupation. This is a natural drainage ditch, hence the autumnal mist. What is more, on reflection the author saw that the coach and horses would have been travelling at an impossible speed in excess of 100mph and has never been considered a true sighting.

The similarities between the two sightings are quite striking.

SPETCHLEY

Ellen Willmott

Unless you are a keen gardener you may never have heard of Ellen Willmott. Ellen appeared at Spetchley Park courtesy of being a distant relative of the owner, John Tasker. Much of the parkland, together with its herds of red and fallow deer, had remained largely unchanged for over 200 years.

By the beginning of the twentieth century John, and his father before him, had amassed a vast collection of plants. Seeking knowledgeable input, he brought in his grandmother, Rose Berkeley, and his great aunt, rose expert Ellen Willmott. By 1914 Ellen had published a work *The Genus Rosa*, featuring an impressive collection of colour prints, which remains one of the leading works on roses today.

Ellen's talents were not restricted to roses; she was renowned for her knowledge with all flora. In particular her habit of surreptitiously scattering seeds of Eryngium, commonly known as Sea Holly, was famous. The seeds remained dormant until the following season when, with a burst of growth, the dome-shaped thistle-like blue flowers appeared as a great surprise to the owner of the garden and the delight of Ellen.

Today, the Eryngium continues to appear magically at the end of the summer, a sure sign that the ghost of Ellen Willmott had paid a visit and scattered the seeds once more.

TARDEBIGGE

Christmas Spirit

Christmas was approaching and everyone in Tardebigge was eagerly awaiting the traditional festive season. A quintessential Dickensian scene would soon be played out by every resident in the village – a walk through the crisp frosty, even snowy, morning in the light of a watery sun to worship at the parish church, followed by as resplendent a meal as most would be likely to sample all year. The promise of goodwill and expectancy of cheer was as invigorating as the day itself.

However, sadly one leading figure in the village would not be present that year for the verger of Tardebigge had suddenly and unexpectedly died. There ensued a heated and decidedly un-Christian argument between the curate and the vicar of nearby Studley, who was standing in at the parish awaiting the appointment of a new permanent vicar to lead the congregation. Both men were adamant they were not going to be the one to bury the poor verger, though for very different reasons. The curate maintained, probably quite rightly, that the onus was on the stand-in vicar and he should be there to conduct the service. However, the first available day for the funeral was the day after the yuletide festivities, which was also the day of the traditional Boxing Day Hunt and the vicar was insisting the responsibility was not his. Neither man was willing to back down and, in an explosion of temper, the enraged vicar felled the curate with a fatal blow.

In a panic the vicar threw the body of the curate in the hearse alongside that of the verger. Under the cover of darkness the vicar buried his still-warm victim in the grave intended for his late colleague, before heading off in the horse-drawn hearse towards Redditch, hiding in the shadows whenever he saw someone approaching, fearful of being discovered. Yet he was seen, by Bill Attewood. The local poacher's furtive exploits were rarely known by anyone, other than those who would later benefit from his activities. Not long afterwards the poacher was found with his head caught in a trap. He was dead.

Since those days the shadow of the ghostly hearse is said to follow that same route it took that Christmas long ago. However, it is considered to be an omen of the worst kind to those who witness it, a warning that they will not be around in twelve months time.

TENBURY WELLS

Fountain Inn

The Fountain Inn is another example of an old country farmhouse refashioned as an ale house. The original seventeenth-century building first served beer and cider in 1855. At this point it was named the Hippodrome in recognition of the horserace track on Oldwood Common next to the inn. For many years it served the drovers as they made their way from the lush pastures of Wales to earn greater profits by selling their livestock in English markets.

Today the excellent menu is supplemented by produce from its home-grown herbs and vegetables. The decor here is unique, boasting a 1,000-gallon tank which holds a dazzling array of marine fish – including the lion fish and a leopard shark (affectionately known as 'Dancer').

However, there is also a resident ghost. What is more the identity of this individual, somewhat unusually, is known. Staff and customers have discovered a glass, a pen, a newspaper, cutlery, condiments, menus, all manner of items mysteriously missing only to be found almost as quickly just an arm's length away. These pranks are never harmful, merely mischievous. That, together with the start date of these pranks, points to one likely individual – Mr Thombs.

The Fountain Inn at Tenbury Wells.

Mr Thombs was the landlord of the inn in the 1950s and he was known as a practical joker. In 1958 a fire broke out in the pub. The landlord waited vital moments to clear the premises and ensure his dogs were saved; as a result he lost his life due to smoke inhalation. Yet it appears that he has returned to keep an eye on the pub he enjoyed running so much.

TIBBERTON

Vindictive Vicar

Towards the end of the eighteenth century the flock attending the Church of St Nicholas were unhappy. During this era the Church still held power over the population and attendance at church, while no longer mandatory, was expected. The local vicar here was engaged in extracting as much money from the people of the parish as humanly possible.

Apparently these monies were urgently required to keep the church in good repair, yet there were suspicions that this was not the case. It was still a relatively small community and the church did not seem to be either receiving or even needing much money spent on its upkeep. Rumours were rife and one evening a few locals got together in the local public house to discuss the matter over several ales. Before the night was done a decision had been reached. It seemed the only solution was to bring about the early departure of the churchman, and the only way to do that was to have him murdered.

However, the gruesome deed was never done. Word of the plot reached the ears of the vicar and he called upon the Church to guard him, warning of the terrible wrath the Almighty would inflict upon the perpetrators from the pulpit at every opportunity. The plotters soon lost their nerve.

The pub reflected the village perfectly, a pious community where the only jobs were in farming and even the inn was named God Speed the Plough. With the weight of the Church behind him the vicar managed to get the reference to God removed from the name of the pub, an ominous message to the superstitious farmers. To this day the pub is still known as simply Speed the Plough.

Eventually the vicar passed away, life in the village continued as normal and regulars still quaffed ale in the pub. Yet within the walls of the pub strange events were reported. A presence loomed over those in quiet conversation, a cold spot here and there, items moving of their own volition, and the sounds of activity in an empty room. Had the vicar, unable to rest in peace owing to his nefarious ways, returned to take his revenge on any who would dare question his integrity?

In living memory little or no activity has been reported, suggesting the troubles of yesteryear have either been forgotten or resolved.

St Nicholas' Church

As with the previous story this tale is centred on the twelfth-century Church of St Nicholas. However, this story does not involve the vicar but one of the parishioners, although which one is a mystery.

St Nicholas' Church is a special place for it has something few English churches have: a wooden tower. Indeed the black and white timber frame is most obvious as it is approached from almost every direction. However, the ghost here is less obvious. She is said to emerge vertically from a grave in the churchyard, however, which grave she comes from is uncertain for different individuals report quite diverse locations. This means her identity is difficult to determine and thus any idea as to why her spirit remains in the churchyard is unknown.

In truth there are not that many headstones in the churchyard and statistically speaking only approximately half of them can be female. Furthermore the sightings have all been on the side of the church where the main gate is, which does reduce the possibilities a little even if this is where the majority of graves are situated. Yet even armed with such deductions there is no clear candidate and any further suggestions would be speculative.

UPTON-ON-SEVERN

Thomas Bound

As the name indicates, the small town of Upton-on-Severn stands on the banks of Britain's longest river. The history of the place is inextricably tied to the river, it being the major transport route for goods from both home and abroad. When the produce could not be brought up by tide and wind in a trow, a two-masted sailing vessel designed to cope with inland waterways was manually hauled by means of ropes held by men walking along the banks. The weight of the fully laden vessel against the swollen river during the winter months must have made this task among the most back-breaking jobs ever.

Perhaps this was one of the jobs taken by Captain Thomas Bound. The infamous Bound is the best known and seemingly most persistent ghost of Upton-on-Severn. During his lifetime he was thought to have committed a number of crimes, the severity of which left his spirit to roam the town for many, many years after his death. A contemporary description of this villainous character was used by Lavender Beard, curator of the museum, to produce a wondrous piece of pottery showing a scene featuring Bound and his horse. The plate is now on display in the museum (*see* Tudor House on page 106).

Bound was said to have married at least three times and two of his wives are thought to have come to unfortunate ends. It is maintained that he killed at least two of them, although he was never brought to justice for his crimes, probably because his misdemeanours were not suspected until after his death. Furthermore while his last wife lay dying in her bed, he is reputed to have forged her will.

Whether it be guilt or punishment for his crimes, his ghost has been seen many times riding his spectral horse through the town. Unlike most ghostly horses this creature does not gallop at speed through the neighbourhood but walks at a sedate pace around the place where Bound himself later committed suicide. At one point, the ghost of Bound became such a problem the clergy were called in to exorcise the unwelcome spirit.

However, this was not the end of the problem. A cat is said to walk the same streets, the pet having belonged to Thomas Bound during his lifetime. After the exorcism Bound's appearances were reported less often, however, his cat is still heard although no record of a sighting has been found. Whether this indicates the two are unrelated is uncertain. Indeed it would not be unusual to find a link between different narratives being created long after they were first mentioned.

The cat was no normal feline. Indeed it must have been instantly recognisable. While many cats have managed to live a normal existence while having just one eye, this one seems to have also managed to get by with only three of its legs. Having four legs the loss of one is certainly less of an inconvenience than those of us who are bipedal. Yet to have given the cat a wooden leg does seem more of a hindrance than a help, especially when it came to hunting prey. The sound of that wooden leg can still be heard clanking along the old streets of Upton. On the quietest of nights one can even hear the cat playing its fiddle – or are these another two stories which have become linked?

White Lion Hotel

The White Lion is a delightful hotel which has been here since at least Tudor times. The impressive frontage is Georgian and the grand covered doorway is supported by white columns and topped by an impressive statue of a lion.

Such a splendid entranceway has welcomed an impressive array of guests over the years including, in recent years, George Sewell and Sir Alec Guinness. However, it is said that one of the most famous actresses ever to tread the boards still walks the halls and corridors of this hotel. Sarah Siddons stayed here when she was touring the theatres around Upton, the White Lion being her preferred hotel. Nobody has ever reported the great actress interacting with anyone or anything in the present hotel, nor is her presence described as anything but friendly.

There are also stories of a cat here, however nobody is quite sure if this is a cat belonging to Captain Bound (*see* previous story). However, the reports would hint at this being a different feline. Firstly nobody has ever heard music which, assuming the fiddling cat is a different entity, would rule this one out. Secondly the cat belonging to Bound has only three good legs, yet the animal at the hotel is felt brushing smoothly past the legs of staff and guests over the years. Thus unless the cat has mastered walking

The splendid frontage of the White Lion Hotel.

on three legs and a wooden stump, and the sound of the cat walking abroad would suggest otherwise, this must be a different creature.

Guests have not been spared by the non-paying visitors to the White Lion. A man staying in room 205 came down for breakfast saying he had been awoken in the night by a feeling of someone in the room. He turned on the light and, although there was nobody there, he felt the very real warm feel of a man's hand shaking his own firmly. This room is the focus for all the reports of ghostly activity upstairs in the hotel.

One couple were staying when the author visited. They reported a definite presence in the same room, which made the husband a little uneasy although his wife was more comfortable remaining in the room. However, the lady did think a number of items had been moved during the night. Another couple from Birmingham make a regular pilgrimage to the hotel. The wife, who has a keen interest in all things psychic, comes specifically to experience the atmosphere, although her husband maintains he is 'only here for the beer'.

Tudor House

Said to be the oldest house in Upton, dating from 1580, Tudor House today houses the Museum of Upton. On the day the author visited he was treated to a private tour by the curator, the wonderful Lavender Beard, whose love for her adopted home town is clearly evident.

The museum has three floors; however, it is the lower two which interest us. Two years ago the museum was visited by a woman who, after completing her visit, announced to the curator that she was a psychic and was she aware of the two resident ghosts. The visitor proceeded to describe how both shades were restricted to one specific area of their particular floor.

About halfway back on the ground floor a male ghost, said to be in period costume, walks back and forth to the saddles which are displayed on the left-hand side. He is thought to be wearing clothes which would put him closer to the earlier period of the building's existence, dating from perhaps the time of the English Civil War. The man appears agitated and paces back and forth, yet says nothing and appears to be unaware of anything going on around him.

Upstairs on the first floor is a bedroom laid out as it would have been in the Georgian or possibly even Victorian eras. Here the woman saw a girl in her early teens. She was wearing a long dress and stands looking around her although, again, her attention is not drawn to anyone around her and she seems quite unaware of the twenty-first century and the museum visitors.

Lavender Beard states that nobody else has ever reported seeing anything, to her knowledge. Furthermore, while there is an undoubted chill in a couple of places, this is not unusual for such an old building. Yet there is Lavender's plate depicting the

The Tudor House may be the oldest building in Upton-on-Severn.

dreadful Captain Bound (*see* page 104), who is shown looking over his shoulder back across the room. Is he aware of something which we are not?

UPTON SNODSBURY

Royal Oak

From 1840 to 1892 three generations of the Bullock family ran the Royal Oak public house, but by the beginning of the twentieth century John Hodges had taken over the reigns. Local stories tell how, somewhere around this time, the head of the household committed an unforgivable and heinous crime.

A young girl, possibly teething or through ill health, was venting her feelings loudly in the only way she knew how. Indeed her crying had been going on for quite some time and the head of the household had grown tired of the girl and, in a fit of rage, threw the child out of the window. She died instantly.

For years later it was reported that, one night every month, the sound of a child crying was heard. The crying is interrupted by a short piercing scream which ends abruptly – then utter silence.

The refurbished Oak, now called The Oak, at Upton Snodsbury.

Upton House

Tucked behind the church dedicated to St Kenelem is Upton House. It is a Norman building with extensive additions from the fourteenth century onwards. However, one recent resident felt sure the ghost of one of their predecessors was still hanging around.

Nobody has ever seen or felt anything, nor has there been any sensation of cold, as is so often reported. Indeed the only clue to the visitor is the smell of tobacco smoke which lingers around the house, and is particularly strong around the front door. The smell of the tobacco is not that with which we are familiar, there is no light gentle aroma the result of a complex and traditional blending of different tobaccos. This is the acrid, pungent raw tobacco smell of yesteryear which dates from possibly as far back as the seventeenth century when tobacco smoking first became popular. The identity of the individual is unknown. However, this is undoubtedly an inquisitive character, for although they normally ignore the modern world, they are quick to react to any change and seem to appear whenever and wherever any visitors arrive or work is undertaken.

Interestingly the person is always described as 'he', yet historically women were pipe smokers too.

Upton House, Upton Snodsbury.

WHITE LADIES ASTON

Low Hill House

Low Hill House is a building with an extraordinarily long and well documented history. The accuracy and longevity of the written history of this place is solely due to its early use as a religious establishment. The first record dates from AD 964 when the Saxon King Edgar gave his approval for an Ecclesiastical Court to be held here. However, the site will have been a point on a route which had already been in use for centuries. Any road named Saltway, which is the name of the track passing the building, shows it was used by those who transported this valuable commodity, possibly since man first settled here.

Over the ensuing years the place, while undergoing a number of changes, also reflected something of British history's significant people and events. The powerful Bishops of Worcester, St Dunstan and St Oswald, stayed here, as did sixteen-year-old Ensign Richard Goodhall Elrington in 1792 while recovering from severe wounds received at Valenciennes while fighting the French Revolutionary Army. Twenty years later, now a Major, he returned with the spoils acquired during action in the Indian Ocean, Arabian Sea and Persian Gulf, including the armour and weapons of the infamous pirate Jo Hasem, which were presented to the city of Worcester.

The Elringtons were an influential family over many generations. In 1802 none other than Admiral Lord Horatio Nelson, often cited as England's greatest ever seafaring hero, stayed here for several nights with his friend Col. Thomas Elrington. Seven years later the colonel died aged eighty-seven, a ripe old age considering the number of times he was wounded during a glittering military career which saw action across much of the northern hemisphere. He was also renowned as the most jovial of characters, even in the heat of battle, and also showed extreme kindness to the people of White Ladies Aston. General Gordon, hero at Khartoum, spent his holidays here when still a schoolboy.

Shortly after the First World War, in 1922, when Ethel Anderson was in residence, she was climbing the stairs to the attic, her way lit by the candle she held, when she came face to face with a very white ghostly apparition. Said to have appeared as a monk, there was not a hint of colour to be seen, indeed Mrs Anderson referred to it as an albino, although this would not explain why the attire was also pure white. It swung slowly from side to side without visible means of support some half a metre above the floorboards. Eventually it faded from view.

Research discovered that, when the building was in use as a school for boys during the reign of King John in the early thirteenth century, there were a couple of deaths here. It was recorded that a monk, having killed one of the schoolboys during a violent rage, then hanged himself by a noose tethered from the rafters of the attic.

WICHENFORD

Wichenford Court

The Washburns were once resident at Wichenford Court. As one of the largest manor houses in the county it would have been an imposing sight for the tenants, with a moat and drawbridge. The place later became a farmhouse, yet, with its wooden panels and carvings, it must have been among the grandest abodes of its kind. Only the dovecote survives, yet even this is a substantial building, today under the control of the National Trust.

Visitors who stayed here in the middle of the nineteenth century reported a number of heads appearing around two sides of a panelled room. The succession of grinning faces resembled carvings, although observers maintained the teeth revealed by those open-mouthed smiles were clearly human teeth.

During the reign of Henry IV there were a number of battles against the uprising Welsh under Owen Glyndwr. At this time a Bourbon prince was held captive at Wichenford, in fact he had been here for some time. His fate was never known but it was rumoured he was murdered under the orders of Lady Washburn. After she died she was spied here again and again. Armed with a dagger, she was either entering or inside the room where the prince was said to have been held and where he died.

A portrait was hung here of another Lady Washburn, whose story has often been confused with that of her earlier namesake; she was the wife of John Washburn, a Royalist and very vocal supporter of Charles I during the English Civil War of the mid-seventeenth century. The confusion is created by the identical name and title of the two women, while they are both said to haunt the building.

From the moat, which can still be made out, on the darkest and quietest of nights the later Lady Washburn has been seen. One cannot fail to recognise her, for she is seen playing a harp of purest gold, seated in a silver boat drawn by four majestic white swans.

WICK

A Plethora of Apparitions

If hauntings are expressed as a percentage of the total population, Wick is the most haunted place in Worcestershire by a distance. Possibly the high number of hauntings in a village of around 600 individuals is the reason why the locals are reluctant to speak of specifics, all I managed to glean was confirmation of the reported clues.

Two grand houses stand on the main street, Wick House and Van Dyke Court, and they are said to have at least one resident ghost each. Twenty-five years ago a cyclist was heading along the path from Pershore, a short straight stretch from near the bridge, when a man appeared quite suddenly in front him. He swerved to avoid the figure and came

Main street at Wick.

off his bike. Jumping up to see if the pedestrian was injured, he discovered there was no one in sight. He had disappeared as fast as he had appeared, and yet the land here is quite open; there are no places to hide without being seen anywhere near the pathway.

However, the most often reported sighting is that of the monks. For years the funeral path to Pershore was taken by everybody, for Wick had no consecrated ground and the only burial ground was in the neighbouring town. The number of monks is remarkable, for they are not only seen individually but also as a procession.

None of my visits to date have treated me to a glimpse of any apparitions while, so far, residents have remained tight-lipped about what has been seen.

WICKHAMFORD

Lady Penelope

Wickhamford is a small community, yet it is easily seen to be a thriving one. A visit to the thirteenth-century Church of St John the Baptist, with its triple-decker pulpit, reveals the Sandys to have been the dominant family in the village until the nineteenth century – the local pub is still known as the Sandys Arms.

The Sandys family monument is on the north side of the church and it is near here we find what we are looking for. One tomb holds the remains of Lady Penelope, not a Sandys but the descendant of a far more famous family. As the translation from the Latin inscription informs us:

> Sacred to the memory of Penelope, daughter of that renowned and distinguished soldier, Colonel Henry Washington. He was descended from Sir William Washington, Knight, of the county of Northampton, who was highly esteemed by those most illustrious Princes and best Kings, Charles the First and Second, for his valiant and successful warlike deeds both in England and in Ireland: he married ELIZABETH, of the ancient and noble stock of the Packingtons of Westwood, a family of untarnished fidelity to its Prince and love to its country. Sprung from such illustrious ancestry, PENELOPE was a diligent and pious worshipper of her Heavenly Father. She was the consolation of her mother, her only surviving parent; a prompt and liberal benefactress of the sick and poor; humble and pure in spirit, and wedded to Christ alone. From this fleeting life she migrated to her Spouse, February 27, Anno Domini, 1697.

Locally she is known as the aunt of George Washington, the first President of America. This family came from Sulgrave in Northamptonshire and is of particular interest to the author. The writer is a first son of a first son for six generations back; the seventh was a first-born daughter, the result of a secret liaison involving a second cousin of the famous American statesman. Thus the grandfather of George Washington is a direct ancestor of the author, making this ghost of Lady Penelope a relative – albeit a distant one – something which could never have been anticipated when embarking on the research.

Wickhamford Church.

A modern monument to
Lady Penelope.

Cow Meadows is the region north of the church and its neighbouring manor house, home to the Sandys, and is cut through by Badsey Brook. Following the First World War, children on holiday from school would gather here to play. Fox and hounds was the favourite game, a variation on hide and seek, as there were so many places to hide. Old trees, sheds, the asparagus at its thickest in late summer proving an effective screen; they would even hide below the banks of the brook when the river was at its lowest.

However, they always hid in pairs for they were very aware that what hid them from view could also hide others from them. At the approach of autumn the wisps of white mist would rise from the waters of the brook, as they thickened they spilled out across the meadows. It was this that warned the children that the games would soon be ending, for they had heard how the mists would form themselves into the ghost of Lady Penelope. She could be seen enjoying her evening stroll around the meadow once more, just as she had in her lifetime during the seventeenth century.

Sandys Arms.

WILLERSEY

Francis's Grave

Along one part of Badsey Lane to the north of the village is said to be a grave. It is known as Francis's Grave, a name which requires a little discussion. Francis was said to be a woman, in which case we would expect the name to be Frances. Alternatively this may have been her surname, which is why it is named Francis's Grave.

Whispered stories have persisted around Willersey for as long as anyone can remember that an old woman from the village, unable to tolerate her suffering a moment longer, took her own life. At the time suicides were excluded from burial in consecrated ground and as such her body was laid to rest on Badsey Lane. Tradition has it that suicides were always buried at a crossroads; however, there is no crossroads or road junction here.

Her ghost is said to wander the roads and fields after dark. Witnesses have described her as being shabbily dressed with a shawl draped around her shoulders. She is noticeably hunchbacked, looks neither left nor right, and appears to have no destination but simply walks slowly on, her demeanour one of abject despair.

Nobody has any notion why she took her own life, nor when, nor exactly where her grave is. If her body should ever be recovered, perhaps it would be a kindness to rebury it in consecrated ground. Perhaps this would finally end the poor woman's suffering and allow her to rest in peace.

WORCESTER

BBC Local Radio

For as long as anyone can recall the studios of the BBC Radio Hereford & Worcester station had been home to more than just the staff. An expert was called in to examine the problem and a number of interesting findings resulted.

It was not long before the investigation reported a 'negative energy' in one studio. A BBC photographer was astonished to discover that a digital photograph taken in the room, a publicity shot of presenter Lindsay Doyle, revealed a strange fuzzy shape which was certainly not present when the image was taken. Furthermore, it was the same corner of the studio in which the presence had been reported.

The building housing the studios is an old one and research, psychic as well as the more usual methods, revealed something of the history. After the Second World War it was used as a tannery. During this period one employee, already known to be suffering from a bout of depression, received a severe dressing down by his boss. He disappeared and was later that day found hanging on an upper floor; he had taken his own life.

An exorcism was adjudged to be the best remedy. Furthermore, it was decided to conduct the procedure live on the Dave Bradley programme. During the broadcast a number of strange noises could be heard, sounds which left the host decidedly unsettled, although the exorcism was proclaimed a total success.

Cardinal's Hat

The Cardinal's Hat is one of the oldest public houses in the county and as such it would be a tragedy if it did not have at least one report of unexplained phenomena. Luckily for the author there have been several.

The building is obviously one of great age. It has that frontage which, while given several facelifts over the centuries, still has the high and narrow façade of an earlier time, and dates from at least the fifteenth century, possibly even earlier. It was known to house the long hooks with which the townsfolk would remove the burning thatch from buildings, which was an effective way of preventing the spread of flames. This link to a fire hazard will prove significant, as we shall see.

The place was serving ale early in the sixteenth century and, although records are incomplete, seems to have done so well-nigh continually since. During Queen Victoria's reign the landlord had a daughter, a girl in her teens, who had long fair hair. At some point during the evening, when the landlord was attending to the needs of his customers in the bar downstairs, a fire broke out on the first floor. No record of the cause exists, if indeed any reason was ever discovered. However, the young girl was trapped and she perished in the fire.

A century later and several managers have reported a number of oddities: items seemingly changing position when their back is turned – a book, a pen, papers, a cup; pictures and other items fell from walls for no reason; barely heard conversations filtered through when the place was empty of customers; sightings of a young blonde woman running away across the first floor landing. All these were said to be the work of the resident ghost.

Several staff members also reported a sudden change in temperature. Always in the upper storeys, no matter what the season, isolated rooms have warmed alarmingly and rapidly. On leaving the room the temperature is found to be normal elsewhere. Is this a flashback to the time when the fatal fire spread through the upper storeys?

Cathedral Bear

In and around the grounds of the cathedral at Worcester, and particularly in the region of College Green, there have been many reports of a ghostly bear.

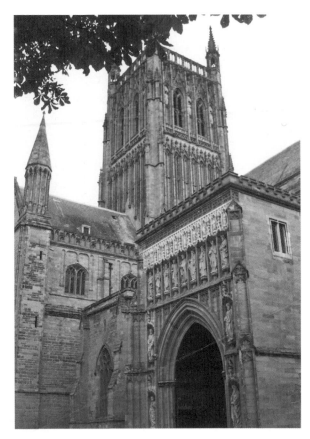

The recently refurbished parts of Worcester Cathedral are obvious.

The first datable record of the sighting comes from the English Civil War. A Parliamentarian soldier, posted to sentry duty on the College Green, was suddenly faced by a huge ursine creature. Terrified, he fired his musket at the animal, yet it had no effect whatsoever. Surely none can be critical of the soldier turning and fleeing his post.

Other reports of the bear are difficult to tie down to a specific period, nor are there specific details. However, one fact stands out in all the reports, the bear is always said to have reared up on its hind legs. Whether this is significant or not is unclear.

Guildhall

Worcester's first guildhall was completed in 1227. Originally a meeting place for merchants, it soon became much more – and continued as a civic administration centre long after the merchant guild, from which it took its name, had disappeared.

The present building is Queen Anne, dating from 1723. It was the work of architect Thomas White, who learned his skills from Christopher Wren, but the city failed to

The splendid Guildhall at Worcester.

settle the bill and the majority of the monies were paid fifteen years after his death, to Worcester Royal Infirmary as demanded in his will. The new building continued to be used for administrative purposes, as indeed it still does to some extent today. The interior also includes three prison cells, built to facilitate the temporary holding of criminals.

All three cells are said to be haunted and have been investigated at length by the local paranormal group. A cell to the south is home to a very strong presence. It has never been seen and, as far as anyone knows, nothing has been heard. However, there is an undoubted temperature drop, far more than should be expected when entering the cell – this is often the first indication of an unseen visitor.

Records of the two other cells have revealed much more information. The cell to the north houses a female ghost, again she has never been seen, but the unmistakable scent of a woman's perfume has been detected. The remaining middle cell has a more gruesome tale to tell. There is a record of a young boy who, desperate to avoid facing the court room, hanged himself in his cell. Several people have reported feeling utter despair when they have stood in this tiny room.

St Helen's Church

The St Helen's Church that we see today stands on the site of what is believed to be the oldest of Worcester's churches; there are indications of its use as a place of worship since the Roman occupation.

Cast by Richard Sanders of Bromsgrove in 1706, the eight bells had a unique set of inscriptions marking the victories of the Duke of Marlborough. They were scrapped after they were removed in 1951, however, it is fitting that they were last heard ringing out to announce the Freedom of the City being conferred on Sir Winston Churchill, a direct descendant of the Duke.

By the end of the Second World War the church no longer held services. It served many uses for the next ten years until, in 1956, the County Record Office occupied the building. Their collection of irreplaceable documents was kept here until 2002, when the present building in Trinity Street took over.

During the forty-odd years as the Record Office, the church was occupied by more people for more hours than at any other period in its existence. Perhaps this was a factor in the frequent sightings of a little girl of approximately eight years of age. She seems to be wearing clothes from the era between the world wars, which would suggest she comes from a time when this was still a place of worship.

Each time she is seen her face is turned to the stone floor, painstakingly examining it as if searching for something small or at least difficult to see. When approached or spoken to, she appears frightened and runs away into the shadows where she vanishes.

As St Helen's is now seeing a revival of its heritage, dedicated to serving the Christian community, perhaps she will be seen again – or maybe the building's return to a spiritual use will allow the girl to rest.

St Helen's Church, Worcester.

Ye Olde Talbot Hotel

Friar Street was named in honour of the Franciscan Friary founded in the first half of the thirteenth century. Nothing is recorded of private housing here for another 200 years. Ye Olde Talbot Hotel on Friar Street, which began life in the thirteenth century, has seen many changes over the years and seen many visitors since its days as a coaching inn.

Two quite separate apparitions have been reported here. The first has always been centred on an upstairs room, number eleven. Over the years this young woman, aged about twenty, has been seen in and around this room, appearing in the traditional clothing of the Quakers, sombre and with little decoration. Most often she appears in the room and disappears out of the window, although recently an employee was approaching the hotel when he saw her leaning out of that very same window.

The girl, who is known as Mary, never interacts with anyone or even seems aware they exist. She is thought to be the girl who died in one of the fires, a constant threat

Ye Olde Talbot Hotel, Worcester.

in a city where most of the buildings were of timber and thatch. For someone who is climbing through a window to save her life she is oddly calm, almost serene in her movements. Perhaps she is recreating her demise, or rehearsing a possible escape to safety which she failed to use when she was alive.

The hotel's second entity is a cat, some describe it as grey and others black, while all report an animal in excellent condition with a glossy coat. During the early twentieth century it was found several times by cleaning staff and maids in rooms which were unoccupied, hence the majority of sightings coming between the hours of 10 a.m. and 11 a.m. As soon as they looked away to summon help, the cat would vanish.

In 2004 the hotel underwent a major refurbishment. As part of the work a recess in the cellar, said to be a tunnel connected to the cathedral, was sealed by a brick wall. Since that time the cat has never been seen.

The Commandery

The Commandery is a Grade I listed building dating from the twelfth century which merits much more than a casual glance. This museum in Worcester has recently undergone a major facelift, bringing to life six distinct periods in the city's history.

This is no ordinary museum; the town's history is told through the eyes of a number of likeable characters who witnessed the events from this very building. Great attention to detail brings these stories to life. In particular, the city's part in the English Civil War reveals much of the men who fought there, while not forgetting those who died there – as we shall see.

When visiting the museum one must keep a watchful eye out so as not to miss a thing. A building of this antiquity should be expected to produce more than what initially meets the eye. This was the case for some particular visitors before the £1.5 million refurbishment, who had their attention abruptly drawn to a clock.

The clock had been part of the exhibition. It had not been hung from the wall, but was resting on a mantelpiece and leaning back against the wall. Those present were mystified when the clock suddenly launched itself from its resting position to crash to the floor and shatter into tiny fragments. It was the trajectory which was most puzzling, for it had not simply fallen but had impacted the floor several feet from where just as if it had been thrown.

A visitor claiming to have psychic abilities reported this room to be home to a marching band of Roman soldiers, this was the first report of any Roman presence. Maybe the legionnaires had knocked the clock from its perch as they passed through? However, the building itself missed the Roman era by over six centuries, while the nearest Roman road is some distance from here. As many see such phenomena as a memory of the past, it seems unlikely that we can blame the Romans for the damage.

The Commandery in Worcester is well worth a visit for history and ghosts alike.

On the tour you will visit the Death and Loss Room. Here is a funeral pall which had belonged to the city and was used at the ceremonies of a number of dignitaries over the centuries. The black cloth was seen as the opposite of the white christening robe, and a black cloth was draped over the coffin while the service was in progress.

The Commandery was purchased by the city in 1973 from David Littlebury, the last of a family who had owned the building for over fifty years. After extensive restoration, taking four years, the building was opened as a museum by the 15th Duke of Hamilton. The choice was not an arbitrary one, the Duke being a descendant of one of the most notable casualties of the Battle of Worcester.

William Hamilton inherited the dukedom by special remainder following his brother James' execution who was beheaded after being found guilty of betraying the land of his birth and his King.

On 3 September 1651 the forces of English and Scottish Royalists loyal to King Charles II met the army of the English Parliamentarians – twice their number. As darkness fell that evening the King's fate was sealed. Of the 31,000 Parliamentarians only 200 lost their lives, but the defeated Royalist forces were in tatters: 10,000 taken prisoner, 3,000 were dead and 2,000 had fled, including the King himself.

During the assault on the city a sortie was led by the 2nd Duke of Hamilton to the north-east out of St Martin's Gate. Within the hour the enemy had driven them back and they were retreating through the city. Among their number was their commander, William Hamilton. He was taken to the Commandery having been shot in the leg. His injuries were treated and he was nursed for the next ten days, but, with gangrene now having taken hold of his wounds, he died.

Since that September day in the seventeenth century his spirit is still said to roam the rooms of the Commandery. Was he responsible for breaking the clock?

Fiveways Hotel

As one can tell by the name, the Fiveways Hotel is situated where five routes converge. Crossroads have, as seen elsewhere in the book, long been considered as haunted spots and this may well be the reason for the reports here.

During the 1980s one witness insisted several quite heavy objects were thrown in his direction. Luckily, the spirit's aim was poor and, apart from giving the potential target a rather nasty shock, there was no actual damage done. However, such aggression appears to have been an isolated event and later reports have been less worrying.

Recently the management allowed a psychic into the building to investigate further, concerned by the increased activity on the top floor. It is here that the living quarters are located and, much to the dismay of the landlady's twenty-one-year-old daughter, the focal point for activity. One day the sound of children playing outside her bedroom door was enough for the young woman to come out into the corridor to point out this part of the building was out of bounds to visitors. Yet when she came out of the room there was nobody to be seen, furthermore a quick review of the security camera records showed nothing.

The Fiveways Hotel, Worcester.

A similar event that happened later seemed to suggest there had been someone outside the living quarters. As the young lady opened the door she saw the heavy fire door was just closing – revealing the recent exit of the trespasser. Anxious to put a stop to these incursions, the images captured by the security camera was replayed. What they saw brought shivers down their spines, for the door had opened but there was no one there. It could not have been opened by the wind as there is no breeze at all in this corridor and there would have to have been a veritable gale blowing along here to move the heavy door.

The psychic investigator has made two or three visits to the hotel and continues to investigate, although no gender, age or era has been suggested – so far.

Fownes Hotel

The large and popular Fownes Hotel overlooking the inner ring road has a history of unexplained events. However, none of these reports have come from the guests, or from the office, bar, kitchen or restaurant staff.

In fact all come from former cleaners and maids, all of whom were employed specifically to clean the guest rooms. The problem for the staff was the unoccupied rooms, those laid out awaiting the arrival of the next guests. Clearly the hotel has a formula, a set routine to be followed by staff where bedclothes are straightened, and

Fownes Hotel, Worcester.

towels, soaps, tea and coffee, etc. were laid out neatly in the accepted eye-catching manner required by the management. With a large number of rooms to be looked after, the staff would be kept busy by the rooms with guests. Thus the odd room which was vacant would require minimal cleaning and tidying – or so they thought.

These empty rooms were sometimes found to be disturbed. Not used or dirty, but the odd towel turned or moved, a cup in the wrong place, a light left on or maybe the radio or television. In these rooms staff sensed an odd presence, described by one former employee as an 'irritation'.

WORCESTERSHIRE

Worcester and Birmingham Canal

The following narrative was related by a man we will call Frank in order to honour his wish to remain anonymous. It concerns one of the two principal canals in the county and one of the tunnels cut on its length through the county of Worcestershire.

Some twenty years ago canals were becoming increasingly popular as leisure sites and the local news reported how volunteers and enthusiasts had cleared another stretch of canal almost every week. As each section was opened up, fish, birds, mammals, amphibians and reptiles were provided with a narrow ribbon of wetland through the conurbations of modern society. They were soon joined by narrowboats making their slow but sure progress at a maximum speed of 4mph, and fishermen, walkers, joggers and cyclists lined the towpath.

It was along this towpath that Frank was ambling one warm afternoon. He freely admits he has never been the fittest of individuals and, as in these early days the towpaths were not given the attention they are today, the journey was not an easy one. Thus he was pleased when he came to the length of tunnel and the cool shade it offered. As with the rest of the route the towpath here was none too even and he had come prepared with a torch to show where he was treading, thus avoiding a stumble and falling into the water. As Frank entered the tunnel he slowed his pace, a sensible precaution considering the dangers, and also kept an eye on what was happening ahead. For reasons he was unable to understand, Frank felt uneasy. He put it down to the dark and dank tunnel but he was under the impression that trouble awaited him. There had been stories of unscrupulous characters hanging around, but nothing concrete had ever been proven.

Having travelled some way into the tunnel, Frank was aware of a boat entering from the other end. He saw the shadow of the boat but noted they had failed to light their headlight, a strange oversight on the part of whoever was steering the vessel. Soon Frank noticed the narrowboat was not getting any closer, indeed it had moored up against the towpath in the tunnel. This was not just unusual, it was quite dangerous too, and Frank was by now fully on his guard and sure that something was amiss. With every sense on heightened alert he slowly closed the gap between him and the end of the tunnel, making sure he also kept a watchful eye on the towpath.

Almost without noticing Frank found himself nearing the end of the tunnel, even the first weak rays of sunlight appeared dazzling after the interminable gloom of the tunnel by torchlight. It was then he realised he missed the boat, he looked around but there was no sign of it, but it could not have had time to pass right through the tunnel. As he emerged into the sunlight he saw two teenage boys fishing, he enquired of them as to what had become of the boat, but they were adamant nothing had passed them and they had been there for a couple of hours.

Was this what had made Frank feel so uneasy? Had he unknowingly sensed this boat was not all it seemed? Since that time Frank has trodden that same path many times, has seen the traffic increase substantially and the towpath resurfaced. The tunnel retains that eerie feeling but, so far, without the reappearance of the boat.

BIBLIOGRAPHY

BOOKS

Bradford, A. *Ghosts, Murders and Scandals of Worcestershire* (Hunt End Books, 2005)
Bradford, A. *The Haunted Midlands* (Hunt End Books, 2006)
Bradford, A. & Taylor, D. *Haunted Holidays* (Brewin Books, 2006)
Bradford, A. & Roberts, B. *Midland Ghosts & Hauntings* (Quercus, 1994)
Bradford, A. & Roberts, B. *Midland Spirits & Spectres* (Quercus, 1998)
Bradford, A. & Roberts, B. *Strange Meetings* (Quercus, 2001)
Drake, D. *History of Bordesley Hall*
Solomon, P. *Ghosts & Phantoms of Central England* (PKN Publications, 1997)
Solomon, P. *Ghosts of the Midlands and How to Detect Them* (PKN Publications, 1990)

NEWSPAPERS & MAGAZINES

Evesham Journal
Kidderminster Shuttle
Worcester Evening Press

Other titles published by The History Press

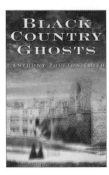

Black Country Ghosts
ANTHONY POULTON-SMITH

Local author Anthony Poulton-Smith takes the reader on a fascinating tour of haunted places in the Black Country. They include the ghost of a murdered woman in Dudley's Station Hotel cellar, the tragic lovers of Cradley Heath's Haden Estate and Walsall's notorious 'Hand of Glory'.

978 0 7509 5044 2

Ley Lines Across the Midlands
ANTHONY POULTON-SMITH

Some maintain that ley lines are the result of some 'earth force', others that they are the earliest routes marked out across the land. In his new book Anthony Poulton-Smith examines the origins and meanings of these ancient trackways, tracing them on foot and taking in markers that have been in existence for millennia to travel in a straight line from Shropshire and Gloucestershire in the west to Cambridgeshire and Lincolnshire in the east.

978 0 7509 5051 0

Haunted Black Country
PHILIP SOLOMON

Compiled by the *Wolverhampton Express & Star's* own psychic agony uncle, Philip Solomon, this selection contains a terrifying range of apparitions; from poltergeists to ancient spirits, silent spectres to historical horrors. Containing many tales which have never before been published, it unearths a range supernatural phenomena, including a ghostly bride who haunts a pub in Walsall; a phantom coach and horses at Kinver; and a Victorian gentleman who appears on a platform at Wolverhampton railway station.

978 0 7524 4882 4

Haunted Birmingham
ARTHUR SMITH AND RACHEL BANNISTER

From creepy accounts from the city centre to phantoms of the theatre, haunted pubs and hospitals, *Haunted Birmingham* contains a chilling range of ghostly phenomena. Drawing on historical and contemporary sources, you will hear about the landlady who haunts the site of her death, the two workmen who died during the building of the Town Hall, the late Mayor who still watches over the city, the last man to be publicly hanged in Birmingham, and many more ghostly goings on.

978 0 7524 4017 0

Visit our website and discover thousands of other History Press books.
www.thehistorypress.co.uk